Making Sustainability Matter

How to Make Materiality Drive Profit, Strategy and Communications

Dwayne Baraka

Email: dwayne.baraka@valuecsr.com

Tel: +44 75 9011 6051

First published in 2014 by Dō Sustainability

87 Lonsdale Road, Oxford OX2 7ET, UK

ISBN 978-1-909293-91-5 (eBook-ePub)
ISBN 978-1-909293-92-2 (eBook-PDF)
ISBN 978-1-909293-90-8 (Paperback)

A catalogue record for this title is available from the British Library.

Dō Sustainability strives for net positive social and environmental impact. See our sustainability policy at **www.dosustainability.com**.

Page design and typesetting by Alison Rayner
Cover by Becky Chilcott

For further information on Dō Sustainability, visit our website:
www.dosustainability.com

DōShorts

Dō Sustainability is the publisher of **DōShorts**: short, high-value ebooks that distil sustainability best practice and business insights for busy, results-driven professionals. Each DōShort can be read in 90 minutes.

New and forthcoming DōShorts – stay up to date

We publish 3 to 5 new DōShorts each month. The best way to keep up to date? Sign up to our short, monthly newsletter. Go to **www. dosustainability.com/newsletter** to sign up to the Dō Newsletter. Some of our latest and forthcoming titles include:

- *The Short Guide to Sustainable Investing*   Cary Krosinsky
- *Strategic Sustainability: Why it Matters to Your Business and How to Make it Happen*   Alexandra McKay
- *Sustainability Decoded: How to Unlock Profit Through the Value Chain*   Laura Musikanski
- *Working Collaboratively: A Practical Guide to Achieving More* Penny Walker
- *Understanding G4: The Concise Guide to Next Generation Sustainability Reporting*   Elaine Cohen
- *Leading Sustainable Innovation*   Nick Coad & Paul Pritchard
- *Leadership for Sustainability and Change*   Cynthia Scott & Tammy Esteves
- *The Social Licence to Operate: Your Management Framework for Complex Times*   Leeora Black
- *Building a Sustainable Supply Chain*   Gareth Kane
- *Management Systems for Sustainability: How to Successfully Connect Strategy and Action*   Phil Cumming

- *Understanding Integrated Reporting: The Concise Guide to Integrated Thinking and the Future of Corporate Reporting* Carol Adams

- *Networks for Sustainability: Harnessing People Power to Deliver Your Goals* Sarah Holloway

Subscriptions

In addition to individual sales of our ebooks, we now offer subscriptions. Access 60+ ebooks for the price of 5 with a personal subscription to our full e-library. Institutional subscriptions are also available for your staff or students. Visit **www.dosustainability.com/books/subscriptions** or email **veruschka@dosustainability.com**

Write for us, or suggest a DōShort

Please visit **www.dosustainability.com** for our full publishing programme. If you don't find what you need, write for us! Or suggest a DōShort on our website. We look forward to hearing from you.

Abstract

MATERIALITY IS A SUSTAINABILITY LYNCH-PIN that binds strategy, the business case and effective reporting together in a way that will result in profitable and effective sustainability initiatives. Many organisations believe that sustainability is important for their success and are committed to becoming more sustainable. But they don't always know how to prioritise action for sustainability, how to get quick wins or how to effectively communicate sustainability programmes to their stakeholders. A well thought out and implemented materiality process can assist organisations achieve all of those things, although getting 'quick' wins will require quite a bit of planning and some sustained hard work. *Making Sustainability Matter* is needed because too many organisations:

- waste resources on sustainability programmes that are not strategically aligned to the organisation,

- do not have optimal returns on sustainability investments,

- do not meet the needs of stakeholders, or

- have programmes that cannot be communicated effectively to generate trust and give transparency that matters.

This guide, penned by business strategy expert Dwayne Baraka, will give readers the tools they need to effectively integrate sustainability into their organisation.

. . . .

About the Author

DWAYNE BARAKA is a career thinker, speaker, facilitator and sustainability expert. Dwayne is committed to monetising 'soft' sustainability disciplines and believes that there are virtually no companies that cannot make their business more profitable through engaging with their most material sustainability issues. As a sustainability professional, he has worked on the corporate strategy of several of the FTSE 100 and many more besides, including tech companies, housing associations, construction companies and others. He has worked in Australia, Bahrain, Belarus, Belgium, Canada, France, Ireland, Latvia, Lebanon, Norway, UAE, USA and UK. He's written award-winning articles on sustainability and has been Editor of the *Encyclopaedia of Corporate Social Responsibility* since 2010. He recently founded valuecsr, a sustainability consultancy focused on executive training, materiality and the business case for sustainability within organisations.

Author Note and Acknowledgements

I WOULD HAVE LIKED TO CALL THIS BOOK 'Sustainability Relevance'. Relevance is useful as a word because it is clear and looks more like the outputs from the process I'm about to lay out for finding the most *relevant* sustainability issues. And it also avoids a word that has other meanings in an organisational context, 'materiality'. The use of that word in the context of sustainability has added to suspicion that corporate social responsibility (CSR) is non-core to business and destroys value. That perception is highly problematic for anyone trying to embed relevant sustainability issues into business process and thinking.

However, the term 'materiality' seems settled among sustainability professionals, and it's more important to improve practice in this area than it is to obsess about nomenclature. I encourage readers to use the word 'relevance' for an internal audience, at least interspersed with use of the 'm' word.

It is my hope that by the end of this book that you will be convinced that a thorough and commercially focused materiality process can set sustainability firmly at the centre of organisational success. My goal is to help make sustainability more like 'just good business'. You might even come to agree with me that materiality is the only sensible basis for organisations to allocate resources for sustainability.

AUTHOR NOTE AND ACKNOWLEDGEMENTS

Of the 5 phases identified, the main focus is deliberately on Scan and Prioritise, while Embed, Manage and Tell are given less focus. For each of the last three parts of the framework, there are some materiality-specific tips, but they are challenges generic to sustainability and they are not covered in depth. The reader should look to other sources (including publications in this series) for additional help.

Thanks to anyone who has ever engaged with me on materiality. Much of what I am now passing on is, in part, yours. Thanks for your wisdom and generosity.

Speaking of which, many thanks to each of the following people who played a direct role in this guide:

- Elaine Cohen
- Eileen Donnelly
- Ian Gearing
- David Grayson
- Rowland Hill
- Thomas Odenwald
- Rachel Parihk

A more brilliant panel of sustainability advisers and reviewers has not been assembled, and it is something of a dream to have their comments on, and input to, this work.

On a final note:

This book is dedicated to Lis and Lincoln, without whose wisdom and generosity this book would not have been possible.

Contents

CONTENTS

Who This Book Is For

THIS BOOK IS RELEVANT PRIMARILY for sustainability professionals who are implementing a materiality process.

More broadly, it is of interest to a range of professionals and other stakeholders who have a professional, personal or academic interest in the relevance of sustainability to particular organisations – its 'materiality'.

The table below offers some guidance for the following audiences.

If you are:	This book will help you:
A sustainability professional	Embed sustainability into business as usual, and begin the journey of calculating the business case for sustainability
An executive	Understand a process for integrating sustainability into organisational strategy, performance and communications
Responsible for sustainability Reporting	To allocate sustainability resources for better reporting and more effective communication with stakeholders
An investor	Understand a business-focused process for identifying material sustainability issues
Tasked with ensuring G4 compliance	Report materiality processes effectively and to the level required to achieve G4 compliance

Navigating this book

The book contains three main types of 'call-out' boxes.

'*Top Tips*' (example right), contains condensed observations and reminders of the most important things to consider in certain areas.

> **TOP TIPS**
> ✓ Observations
> ✓ Reminders

'*Tips for Advanced Companies*' (example below), is meant for more sophisticated readers, or readers who are re-visiting the guide after implementing a materiality process.

> **TIPS FOR ADVANCED COMPANIES**
> Notes for more sophisticated readers. Also, additional tips for companies who already have an established materiality process.

Each part also has a checklist at the end (example below). Only the bravest and most creative among us should attempt to use the checklists without first reading the relevant content. Readers who like to have a clear map before setting off can skip to the end of each part to the checklist to see what's coming!

> **CHECKLIST**
> ☐ Step 1 – Read section content before using
> ☐ Step 2 – Use this Checklist

Unique definitions

There are a few definitions that will be consistently used in this book, as follows.

- **Sustainability Issue Record (SIR)**
  - Long list of sustainability issues that could be relevant to your business

- **Material Sustainability Issues (MSIs)**
  - Short list of the most relevant sustainability issues

- **Sustainability Team**
  - The formal sustainability team in your organisation

- **Special Advisers**
  - A group of advisers or champions who assist with the materiality process, but aren't part of the Sustainability Team

For reference purposes, a few of the more common acronyms are also included here:

GRI Global Reporting Initiative

SASB Sustainability Accounting Standards Board

IIRC International Integrated Reporting Council

PART 1

What, Why and Who

What?

Defining materiality

THERE ISN'T A WIDELY-AGREED DEFINITION of materiality in relation to sustainability. The working definition of materiality for this guide is:

> *The relevance of each sustainability issue, taking into account the effect of each issue on the organisation and on its stakeholders.*

Most companies engaging with materiality adopt working titles for those effects, something like 'Importance to Stakeholders' and 'Impact on Organisation'.

Materiality of each issue is often thought of (and reported) relative to other sustainability issues. However, there is increasingly a drive to report sustainability issues alongside other organisational issues, especially through Integrated Reporting. We will look at the significance of that later, but first, we need to contrast the definition of materiality in sustainability to other uses in organisations.

How it's different in sustainability

In law and accounting, 'materiality' is used in relation to disclosing certain circumstances with a threshold financial consequence, usually in relation to public disclosure for listed companies or merger/acquisition activity. Failure to report circumstances that reach the threshold carries some (often dire) negative consequences.

In the legal/accounting realm, materiality is usually defined with clear, absolute markers; often tagged to a quantifiable threshold of revenue or costs. For example, it may be defined as 5% of total revenue, meaning that if an event isn't likely to result in a decrease in revenue of 5%, then it need not be disclosed. Such percentage thresholds are often a function of pragmatism within accounting firms.

In sustainability, the term 'materiality' is a relative term with fluid boundaries, flexible to organisational strategies and currently the subject of some disagreement. In practice, it is about relevance and prioritisation of sustainability issues, and sustainability professionals need to be ready to expound the difference between legal/accounting materiality and the sustainability materiality process they are proposing or using.

Companies have infrequently disclosed sustainability risks as material risks in the legal/accounting sense of that word. In 2013 Coca-Cola became the first company to disclose a sustainability risk in its compulsory Form 10-K filed with the Securities and Exchange Commission. It is difficult to overestimate the significance of the filing of that particular form to the perception of importance of sustainability issues to the wider business community. That example shows that one of the ways to highlight the value of a sustainability materiality process is to connect it to other organisational processes, including the processes involving traditional materiality. There are probably many more risks on a corporate risk register than meet the legal meaning of materiality, and that will give you some leverage in relation to CSR issues.

When it comes to sustainability issues, you should be clear that you aren't necessarily saying that they need to be disclosed in the annual report as legally 'material', but that the issues *may* impact on the organisation in a way that the organisation needs to know about. If you've really done your homework on your organisation's sustainability issues, you will have an idea of the quantum of impact the issues can have on the organisation. If you can turn that into a number, then you are very likely to grab attention.

The challenge of traditional materiality

Traditional concepts of materiality can mean that organisations underachieve on issues that are below materiality thresholds in two ways.

First, organisations can ignore issues that are outside the (rather arbitrary) materiality limits. That means that they are not creating as much value as they could.

Figure 1 illustrates this problem. The issues in the unshaded area are not 'material' (in the legal/accounting sense), but they still create or destroy significant amounts of value for organisations.

Second, many of the 'business-as-usual' Organisational Issues will be included in organisational processes, but Sustainability Issues might be ignored. Organisations ignoring sub-'material' sustainability issues do so at their own peril, especially because the sum of those issues is often a very large number in aggregate.

FIGURE 1. Traditional materiality threshold illustrated.

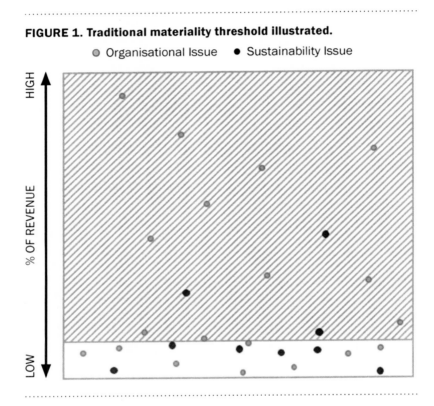

TIPS FOR ADVANCED COMPANIES

GRI's implied definition of materiality is useful for companies more focused on meeting stakeholder expectations. It is:

Aspects of sustainability that:

- *reflect the organisation's significant economic, environmental and social impacts; or*

- *substantively influence the assessments and decisions of stakeholders*

Many organisations use "Impact on the Business" instead of the first bulleted point above. GRI's approach is fundamentally different and broader ranging.

Most companies will benefit from understanding that distinction, particularly companies that:

1. have high transparency requirements,

2. wish to be known as leaders on sustainability issues, and/ or

3. apply the precautionary principle in relation to sustainability issues.

SustainableBrands has an interesting article on the effect of differing definitions of materiality: **http://www.sustainablebrands. com/news_and_views/articles/are-materiality-matrices-really-material**

Why?

Expectations of inclusion of an analysis of materiality of sustainability issues in corporate reports have increased, partly due to the inclusion of a materiality process into the main corporate reporting frameworks: GRI's G3 and more recently IIRC's Integrated Reporting framework. Global companies are reporting record levels of identification of material

FIGURE 2. KPMG's Survey of CR Reporting: self-reported identification of material issues.

Does the report identify material issues? Sector view.

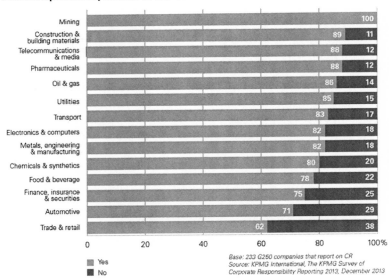

Base: 233 G250 companies that report on CR
Source: KPMG International, The KPMG Survey of Corporate Responsibility Reporting 2013, December 2013

SOURCE: http://www.kpmg.com/Global/en/IssuesAndInsights/ArticlesPublications/corporate-responsibility/Documents/corporate-responsibility-reporting-survey-2013.pdf

sustainable issues (Figure 2), but the basis of that estimation is called into question by a stark lack of frequency of a formal materiality process, with only 23% of those companies declaring that they have a regular materiality process in place (Figure 3).

FIGURE 3. KPMG Survey of CR Reporting: company assessment of materiality.

How often do companies assess material issues?

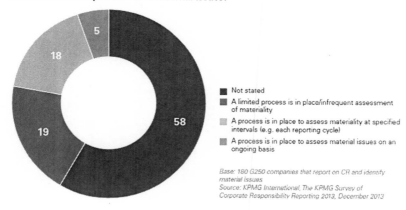

■ Not stated
■ A limited process is in place/infrequent assessment of materiality
■ A process is in place to assess materiality at specified intervals (e.g. each reporting cycle)
■ A process is in place to assess material issues on an ongoing basis

Base: 180 G250 companies that report on CR and identify material issues
Source: KPMG International, The KPMG Survey of Corporate Responsibility Reporting 2013, December 2013

SOURCE: http://www.kpmg.com/Global/en/IssuesAndInsights/ArticlesPublications/corporate-responsibility/Documents/corporate-responsibility-reporting-survey-2013.pdf

Further, shareholders are also more active than ever (see Figures 4 and 5), filing more resolutions in relation to sustainability and voting in favour of them more often. That is certainly true in the US, where such information is readily available. The data on the UK and EU lags behind the US, but anecdotal evidence suggests a similar trend.

FIGURE 4. Shareholder support in US for ESG proposals.

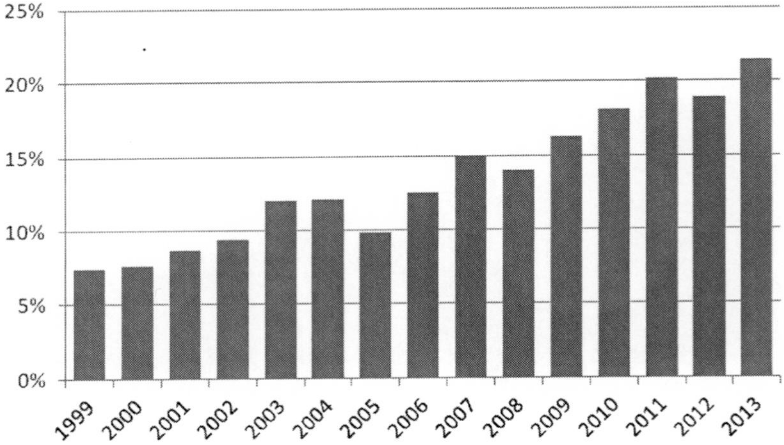

SOURCE: http://www.issgovernance.com/files/private/2013ISSUnitedStatesPostseaso nReport.pdf

As a result of the increased focus on relevant sustainability issues, organisational processes need to find ways to accommodate the new landscape. GRI's G4 reporting framework requires much more comprehensive disclosure of a corporate materiality process, and it seems that expectations of materiality disclosures will only increase.

FIGURE 5. Social/environmental proposals filed in US in 2013.

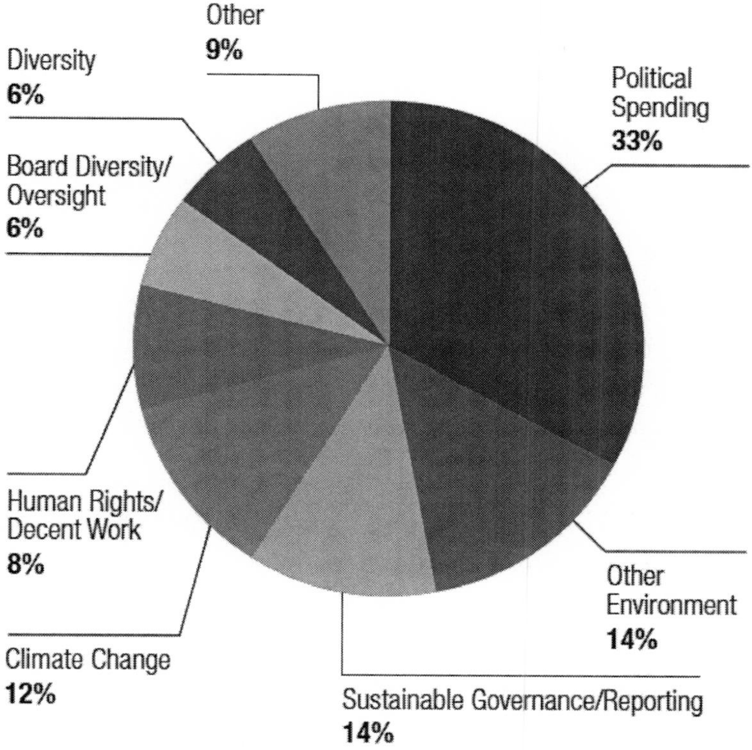

Other
9%

Diversity
6%

Board Diversity/
Oversight
6%

Political
Spending
33%

Human Rights/
Decent Work
8%

Other
Environment
14%

Climate Change
12%

Sustainable Governance/Reporting
14%

SOURCE: http://www.proxypreview.org/#about

Purpose of a materiality process

The main purpose of the materiality process outlined here is to put sustainability issues inside usual organisational processes; to make sustainability part of doing good, profitable business. That will necessarily involve identifying and prioritising issues that have otherwise fallen between business-as-usual cracks.

The above factors all add external pressure to include a materiality process in sustainability reporting. But there are many company-based reasons to institute a materiality process.

Business case

Identifying the most important aspects of sustainability can help organisations allocate resources for sustainability impact. If done well, a materiality process will identify the most important sustainability issues which in turn will add the most value (or reduce the most risk) from sustainability.

A good materiality process will also implicitly identify things to start measuring to calculate a business case for sustainability. However, making the business case requires measurement, and committing resources to measuring often requires proof of the business case. Intuitive consensus, backed and tested by rigorous measurement, seems to be a way out of this catch-22, although a certain amount of consensus (or authoritarian directive) will be required.

One company that is measuring its sustainability business case is Marks & Spencer (see Case Study, below).

Communications

The outputs from a materiality process become inputs to a good communications strategy. All of the most relevant issues to stakeholders should be addressed, especially if the company is giving priority to a limited set of issues, more so if an organisation needs to convince investors that it has already thought about creating and sustaining value in the long run.

> **With so many ESG topics to consider, organisations are often persuaded into pursuing pet programs that . . . appease management but fail to address core business impacts**[1]

Cultural implications

Materiality processes can drive understanding of sustainability and profoundly affect organisational culture. Showing the relevance of sustainability issues can have an effect on staff behaviour that further embeds organisational values.

Strategic connections

Organisations that do not adequately understand sustainability will not survive the changes of the future. Sustainability is becoming increasingly connected to core operations. A thorough materiality process will help organisations identify areas where their practice needs to change and, more importantly, where new strategic opportunities are arising.

That's particularly true for organisations that want to be seen as sustainability leaders, but even organisations that want to adopt a mid-market or slightly lagging position on sustainability will benefit from insights into burgeoning sustainability issues and hearing directly from relevant stakeholders.

CASE STUDY: Marks & Spencer

Sustainability at M&S

Marks & Spencer (M&S) has responded to social needs since it was founded. In 1884 the company evidenced its strong social conscience by championing good employment conditions. It has been involved in CSR initiatives ever since.

Following the launch of Plan A in 2007 (a £200m. investment in sustainability) there was greater emphasis on the environment and health & wellbeing throughout business processes and products. Plan A was designed to address all the key social and environmental issues relevant to a retailer and position M&S as a sustainability leader. It has learnt much since starting its journey.

M&S Materiality Process

M&S now follows a four-stage materiality process.

Stage 1 – Assessing stakeholder priorities:

Its wide ranging process takes into account customer, employee, supplier, investor, political and NGO priorities. The Plan A team is often the catalyst for collating results at a particular point in time (which provides a common point of reference), but business units engage with stakeholders on their priorities at various times throughout the year.

The process is co-ordinated by the Plan A team but feedback from each group of stakeholders remains 'owned' by the relevant business unit and uses a wide range of mechanisms such as employee surveys and feedback from meetings. The Plan A team owns only a few relationships, and people in the business are now comfortable with receiving an introduction to stakeholders of interest.

Specific ownership is important because it educates business owners and builds relationships with stakeholders most closely related to relevant business functions. Examples of relationships that were initially established by the Plan A team and then passed on to business owners include:

- the ethical trading (procurement) teams working directly with Oxfam, Christian Aid and others,

- food agronomists working closely with the Pesticides Action Network, and

- property teams working with the UK Green Building Council.

To build trust, M&S annually publishes the main results of its engagement (Table CS1.1, below).

TABLE CS1.1 – Stakeholder engagement conclusions

OUR STAKEHOLDERS	HOW WE LISTEN	SO THIS IS WHAT THEY'VE TOLD US
Customers	• Monitoring sales of products • Offering involvement in Plan A activities and campaigns • Receiving feedback through our Retail Customer Services team • Feedback through our Plan A suggestions email • Conducting research and surveys • Making increasing use of Facebook and Twitter social media	Environmental and social issues continue to be important but our customers have other pressures and priorities. They want to buy products that offer high standards in all respects and have the opportunity to contribute to causes which are important to them.
Employees	• Plan A Champions in all locations • Business Involvement Groups • Feedbaack through our Plan A suggestions email • Annual You Say survey • Involvement in a wide range of Plan A activities • Plan A listening groups	Many of our colleagues want us to continue to cut waste, help local communities and communicate better to our customers.

OUR STAKEHOLDERS	HOW WE LISTEN	SO THIS IS WHAT THEY'VE TOLD US
Shareholders	• Annual General Meeting • Meetings with institutional investors • Surevy of institutional investors • Ethical investment strategy	Investors are increasingly interested in how Plan A contributes to the success of our business and how this should be measured.
Suppliers	• Annual Plan A Supplier Conference • Tendering processes • Supplier Exchange • Visits and meetings • Agricultural shows	Our suppliers are looking for M&S to adopt an holistic approach to sustainability which reflects developing industry-wide standards.
Government and regulators	• Meetings • Dialogues with trade associations • Responses to consultations • Annual Plan A Stakeholder Conference	EU and UK goverment have been developing proposals to improve corporate accountability on social and environmental issues through reporting. We have attempted to incorporate many of these proposals into this year's reports.

OUR STAKEHOLDERS	HOW WE LISTEN	SO THIS IS WHAT THEY'VE TOLD US
Non-governmental organisations (such as WWF, Oxfam, RSPCA, Greenpeace and Friends of the Earth)	• Visits and meetings • Participation in benchmarking and surveys • Joint projects • Annual Plan A Stakeholder Conference	NGOs want M&S to continue to show leadership and collaborate with other companies to help bring changes across the whole industry

Stage 2 – Risk / Opportunity assessment

A bi-annual risk and opportunity assessment is conducted with the help of the Internal Audit and Risk Assessment team.

The stakeholder priorities gathered in Stage 1 are used as an input to develop understanding of risks and opportunities for M&S.

It results in two levels of risk assessment: the principal risks and uncertainties which are detailed every year in the Annual Report and the more detailed specific 'non-financial' risks and opportunities, which are often contributory factors to the principal risks. For example, many individual social and environmental supply chain uncertainties contribute to its wider ability to provide high quality products.

Results of the biannual process are reported to the Board. They manage identified risks, often telegraphing their mitigation strategy, as in Figure CS1.1, below.

FIGURE CS1.1 – M&S Risk Assessment

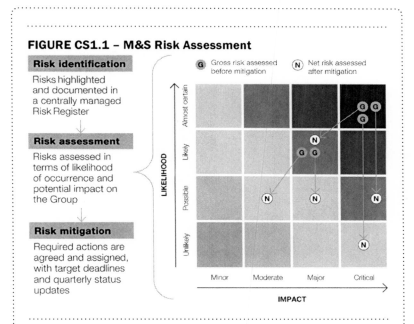

Risk identification

Risks highlighted and documented in a centrally managed Risk Register

Risk assessment

Risks assessed in terms of likelihood of occurrence and potential impact on the Group

Risk mitigation

Required actions are agreed and assigned, with target deadlines and quarterly status updates

Some issues identified represent only a risk to the business, but the same process identifies opportunities.

Stage 3 – Gap Analysis

After stakeholder priorities and strategic risks and opportunities have been gathered, M&S uses a spreadsheet to list all issues, compare them to current activities and identify any gaps. New issues emerge (or expectations have moved) and M&S sometimes finds it isn't doing enough to meet stakeholder or business expectations. The gap analysis helps to revise targets in order to ensure that Plan A remains relevant and provides a leadership position.

Its materiality process has helped it to identify additional Plan A commitments, up to 180 in 2013 from the initial list of 100 in 2007.

Plan A

CERTIFIED CARBON NEUTRAL® company

CO₂ neutral
We were proud to retain our status as a certified CarbonNeutral® company across our operations in the UK and Republic of Ireland. We are actively developing programmes aimed at encouraging our suppliers to reduce their greenhouse gas emissions.

Plan A products
45% of our products now have a Plan A quality – such as Fairtrade, organic or made from recycled material. We're making good progress against our target of making this 50% of products by 2015.

45%

Stage 4 – Benchmarking

To ensure that M&S remains a leader in the retail sector, it regularly benchmarks current performance and targets against competitors and other leading companies outside the retail sector.

That process highlights how issues have developed since previous benchmarks and whether M&S needs to adopt a more ambitious approach.

Outputs

The resulting output of the four-stage process is a matrix of issues plotting importance to stakeholders and importance to M&S (Figure 15, p.112).

The Materiality Matrix is compatible with the processes outlined in GRI's G3 and G4 and supplements GRI's 'off the peg' list of issues with the M&S defined universe of issues. This key difference between M&S's process and the GRI G3 approach is that it tends to identify lots of product and supply chain retail impacts that G3 doesn't include and excludes certain other issues.

Although M&S doesn't publicly disclose the full Materiality Matrix, it uses the grid to determine levels of assurance needed in order to give appropriate levels of confidence in the data it gathers.

How M&S Embeds its Materiality processes

M&S expects that the process of materiality assessment will become increasingly important in improving the relationship of non-financial information contained in both Annual Reports and Sustainability Report. It sits at the heart of IIRC's draft Integrated report framework, GRI G4 and the UK's new regulation on narrative reporting.

The resulting programmes, targets and monitors form the backbone of internal management systems and reporting of performance to a wide range of audiences.

Materiality processes have already helped identify sustainability as one of the best business investments it has made (Figure CS1.3, below). It has resulted in KPIs for the whole business which reduce costs and helped make its whole product portfolio and strategy more sustainable.

FIGURE CS1.3 – M&S Plan A Net Benefit

Net Benefit

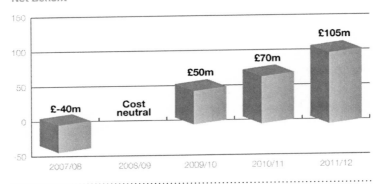

Lessons for Others

M&S found that this process works best if there is a clearly stated and bold ambition right at the start and from the top.

Before Sir Stuart Rose defined his ambition for M&S as a leader with 'clear blue sky between M&S and its competitors', predecessor programmes to Plan A often resulted in decisions determining that performance within an 'industry average' band was sufficient. That meant it didn't inspire its people to innovate for sustainability.

People came to expect a lot of M&S because of its stated ambition to be a leader, which could have been a danger. But ultimately that was helpful because it motivated staff to innovate and its stakeholders now help M&S innovate and achieve a leadership position. The gap analysis in particular helped it to realise that targets weren't aligned with the desired leadership position, which had been creating challenges internally when a Director had expectations of winning awards on an issue – yet the relevant performance target was to sit within a market average.

M&S now innovates to retain its leadership position.

Who?

A mixture of internal and external people will make your materiality process a success. If you don't have a Sustainability Team, add forming one to your to-do list.

Internal stakeholders

If you have an established Sustainability Team, let them know what you are doing and use this guide as a checklist to ensure you have the right people on the Sustainability Team. Add to the team where it can add value to this process or, if that isn't possible, ask them to be Special Advisers.

A good team will usually include a representative from each main part of the organisation. A variety of organisational levels can be useful because of the varied perspectives. Functions represented should include:

- **Communications** – Communications can help to create trust (both internally and externally), especially in relation to community perceptions and the overall effect of sustainability on brand value.

- **HR** – HR teams are usually heavily involved in functions with strong connections to sustainability including training, workplace culture, well-being of employees, recruitment, diversity and internal communications.

- **Procurement** – Procurement staff know a lot about how your organisation makes buying decisions and can influence inputs into the organisation. Their participation is especially important in relation to sustainable supply chain issues, which are increasing in importance.

- **Sales and Marketing** – As the primary relationship owners of your organisation's customers, and representatives of your organisation's brand, Sales and Marketing staff need to be represented in relation to materiality. They are also the closest to pre-qualification and tendering processes and may be the first to know that comparative sustainability practice is lacking.

- **Risk and Compliance** – The Risk and Compliance function are very often part of the creation of organisational dashboards that drive behaviour throughout the organisation. Their knowledge about numbers will also be invaluable!

- **Customer Service** – Customer Service staff are often the front-line when things go wrong. Having them involved gives a direct perspective from an important stakeholder.

- **Operations** – Operations staff are the engines of efficiency of organisations and can add useful insights to the Sustainability Team and also implement some widespread changes. Take some time to understand the Operations function; if it is diverse, you might want to have several representatives if they perform sufficiently different functions. Some organisations include other functions (such as health, safety and environment) within this team.

- **Finance** – You'll need someone who understands spreadsheets in a way that probably currently mystifies you. They can help out on things like return on investment (ROI) analyses and other core finance skills.

- **Health and Safety** – Although health and safety can be an engine for legal compliance, they can also assist with various aspects of employee skills, motivation, well-being and engagement.

- **Environment** – The environment team play a relatively obvious role. Some organisations successfully use their environment team's work as a basis for internal and external engagement campaigns.

- **Strategy** – Any Sustainability Team that doesn't have the involvement of the team in charge of organisational strategy will perennially struggle to embed change flowing from the materiality process. Ideally that would involve a senior member of the Strategy team.

If your organisation has other units or teams not listed above, consider whether they can affect or will be affected by your organisation's reputation, trust or perception of sustainability. If they will, then they should be involved. They should also be involved if they 'own' relationships with influential or key stakeholders.

It is important, if possible, to have highly-ranked managers and at least one Director involved in the materiality process. That's because the connection between sustainability, values and strategic management is profound. When selecting a top-level representative, it is probably more important to find someone who is actively supportive of sustainability than it is to have the highest profile candidate.

External stakeholders

In order to prioritise stakeholders you will need to gather a list of who they are! You should be identifying the stakeholders that influence your organisation and also those that are influenced by it. It might be helpful to use some questions for that process:

- Who is affected by the organisation's bottom line?

- Who affects the opinions of customers and business partners?

- Who can affect the future viability of the organisation?

List as many external stakeholders as you can think of from the list in Table 1 and identify the stakeholders that you think have the highest ability to influence your organisation. Get the views of the Sustainability Team, especially those from Senior Management.

Your organisation is likely to have more stakeholders than are listed in Table 1, and as your materiality process expands, you should be talking to more of your stakeholders, and fragmenting groups based on issues that they are concerned about. Plan to include your most important stakeholders and consider when to involve others. It is important to identify stakeholders that are only relevant for one business unit or function, even though in aggregate they may not be the most influential.

Be alert to the tendency to discount or ignore the perspective of uncomfortable or antagonistic external stakeholders. Marginalising them can escalate their behaviour and issue. It also alienates the organisation from the groups who are most active in driving discussion of the issue. Many organisations have found that very useful insights come from stakeholders with more demanding perspectives, which lead to more robust and useful internal discussion of relevant issues.

Next, identify who each of your Sustainability Team's most important external stakeholders could be, and ask the Team to review this. Perhaps use the same questions with them as you asked above.

TABLE 1. External stakeholders to consider

STAKEHOLDER	CORE VALUE	PERSPECTIVE
Customers	Can tell you what they think about sustainability, and what sort of new products or services they want.	• Product offering • Sustainability hygiene factors • Trust in organisation • Making sustainability easy
Trade/industry Bodies	Perspective on direction of travel of the industry or sector	• Identify expected minimum levels of sustainability • Benchmarking
Suppliers	Need to help preserve your reputation by having similar sustainability values to you	• Grassroots business activity • Possible areas of innovation
Business critics	Can highlight the areas of sustainability that will generate negative press coverage	• Negative externalities • Reputation
Government	Identify possible regulatory changes	• Regulatory and compliance risks (and opportunities)
Shareholders	Identifying demand for sustainability metrics	• ROI/business case for sustainability
Environment	Organisational use of, and reliance on, the environment (natural capital)	• Cost base for resources • Compliance costs • Future profit opportunities
Local communities	Need to maintain a local licence to operate (legal and social)	• Value to community • Local issues • Needs of local communities

STAKEHOLDER	CORE VALUE	PERSPECTIVE
Development agencies/NGOs	Identify wide-ranging social needs, which your organisation may be able to address	• Generation of shared value • 'Licence to operate' • Emerging issues • Justice campaigns
Media/business commentators	Connecting sustainability issues to brand and business value generated	• Reputation • Trust • Brand value
Employees	Whether you are living up to your values and stated objectives	• Source of innovation • Engagement equals productivity gains

NOTE: This table is not meant to be an exhaustive list!

Using proxies and facilitators

Proxies

Using representatives to speak on behalf of external stakeholders can be a cost-effective way to include external stakeholders, particularly when getting started with materiality. But DO NOT make the mistake of finding proxies before identifying relevant stakeholders.

The best representatives will be experts who are familiar with relevant areas of sustainability (including sustainability reporting and good practice) and have an informed point of view on your company's sustainability strengths and weaknesses. Their insights can help minimise any overly positive or unrealistic self-assessments by your organisation and help you to minimise the hype-cycle that can occur.

However, nothing replaces direct dialogue with a stakeholder. Conversations with proxies do not directly create trust with the stakeholders nor allow internal sceptics to see that external stakeholders are reasonable people with valid concerns.

Facilitators

Using consultants or sustainability experts can be useful when talking with stakeholders. They can have more candid conversations and encourage more open dialogue than an 'insider', which in turn creates greater trust in your organisation. They may also be useful in internal conversations by keeping focus on sustainability issues, avoiding getting lost in internal political issues and moving sustainability conversations forward much faster.

CHECKLIST: PART 1 – What, Why and Who

WHAT

☐ Be comfortable with a definition of materiality

☐ Be able to confidently articulate the difference between legal/accounting materiality and sustainability materiality

WHY

☐ Understand and be able to articulate the connections of materiality to business value and processes

☐ Know which aspects of WHY are most important to your organisation

WHO

- ☐ Identify which Internal Stakeholders will be involved
- ☐ Form a Sustainability Team (if there isn't one already)
- ☐ Identify which External Stakeholders can add the most value first time around and others who will be more valuable in the future
- ☐ Check your conclusions with the Sustainability Team
- ☐ Consider using proxies and facilitators
- ☐ Invite the Internal and External Stakeholders to be part of the materiality process

PART 2

How

THIS PART UNPACKS A MODEL MATERIALITY PROCESS for determining
and integrating material sustainability issues (Figure 6).

It would have been nice to come up with *the* definitive materiality process.
Be sceptical of anyone who says they have – the reality is that organisations

....

FIGURE 6. Materiality process.

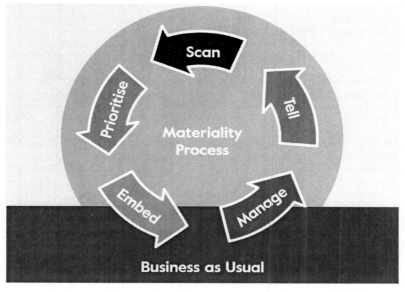

will need to modify any standard process in ways that work for them. If you modify this model to fit your organisation, please let me know what you did!

SCAN

The first substantive task is to scan for relevant sustainability issues. This process should identify things relevant for the organisation now, and also capture burgeoning and future issues. It is sensible to identify a wide array of sustainability issues – a long list at an early stage is almost never a disadvantage.

Materiality processes should use one or more sustainability frameworks as a reference point and also an organisation's view of itself.

Sustainability frameworks

There are several sustainability frameworks that can inform your scan. Each has its own relative strengths and weaknesses. The frameworks are usually externally constructed, and do not always reflect organisational language or understandings. When selecting one, look for cues from the language used in the framework, the organisation's current understanding of its role in society and your own intuition.

Don't sweat on the selection too much – most frameworks can add a degree of value, particularly as a lens for scanning for sustainability issues. In any case, there is no shame in changing frameworks at some time in the future; it may add value as sustainability strategy matures.

The major frameworks are discussed below. Others are available (including ISO 26,000, OECD Guidelines, UNGC and EU guidelines) but are not included as they don't easily accommodate materiality. However, if they have currency in your organisation, you should consider using them. You may also want to review the UN's Business & Human Rights framework if you have operations in more than one country.

Further explanation of each of the main models appears below. If you already know which model to use, or have a framework that your organisation already uses, skip to Identifying issues, *p.63.*

Capitals

The basic capitals model has been around for several years,[2] but has become more prominent recently through use by the International Integrated Reporting Council, the Global Initiative for Sustainability Reporting and the Sustainability Accounting Standards Board in their respective frameworks. Two main capitals models now exist, and although the difference between them is small, the language used is quite different.

Five Capitals

The Five Capitals model consists of five types of 'resources' or capitals that our society needs to function well. Analysis of capital occurs at a very high level and the organisational connection is the contribution to or reliance on each of the capitals.

Natural capital is any physical material (including derived energy) that produces goods and services. Examples are:

- resources such as oil and timber,

- 'sinks' that absorb, neutralise or recycle wastes (such as growing forests, which absorb atmospheric carbon) and

FIGURE 7. Five Capitals Model

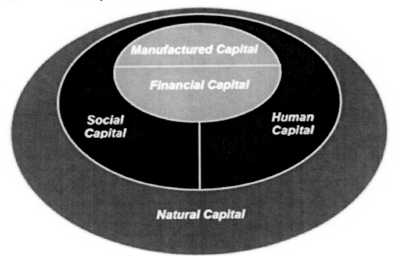

SOURCE: http://www.forumforthefuture.org/project/five-capitals/overview

- environmental regulations (which are a process but part of the overall calculation).

Human capital is all the things needed for humans to produce output, for example, health & safety, knowledge, skills and motivation. Training usually increases human capital.

Social capital is resources created by social institutions that maintain and develop human capital, including collaboration, for example, families, communities, trade unions, clubs, schools, NGOs, corporate entities.

Manufactured capital is fixed assets used in production processes, for example, tools, machines and buildings.

Financial capital is representational measures (e.g. money) that enable other types of capital to be owned and traded.

....

FIGURE 8. Six Capitals Model

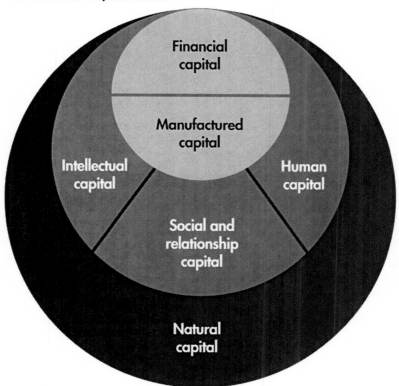

SOURCE: http://www.theiirc.org/wp-content/uploads/Consultation-Draft/Consultation-Draft-of-the-InternationalIRFramework.pdf

....

Six Capitals

The International Integrated Reporting Council (IIRC) has adopted a Six Capitals variation on the Five Capitals model. 'Knowledge' is removed from Human capital and becomes the sixth category, Intellectual capital (see Figure 8). The IIRC's model looks at capitals generated or used by an organisation.

Intellectual capital is knowledge accumulated by an organisation.

The model is written in more business-friendly language than the Five Capitals.

TIPS FOR ADVANCED COMPANIES

Some effort has gone into valuing Natural Capitals recently, perhaps the most high profile of which is Puma's Environmental Profit and Loss Report, first published in May 2011. Although it is methodologically fraught with difficulties, compromises and estimates, it still makes for interesting reading. **http://about.puma.com/puma-completes-first-environmental-profit-and-loss-account-which-values-impacts-at-e-145-million/**

Another example is the valuation of trees by UK's The Guardian newspaper, published in infographic form. That puts the purely economic value of trees as a commodity at £400m, while their systemic environmental value is £3,700m. **http://www.theguardian.com/sustainable-business/graphic/what-is-natural-capital-infographic**

It is important to understand that the Puma model and the

---

valuation of trees deal with only one aspect of Natural Capital. A thoroughgoing Capitals Model analysis is very broad-ranging and well beyond the reach of many organisations. It is also possible to take something of a hybrid approach, blending the Capitals and other frameworks, as shown in Appendix D.

ESG, SEE, PPP, CEMW

These frameworks have much in common, and choosing between them may be a matter of choosing the words that most closely align to current business language.

Environmental, Social & Governance (ESG)

This is the framework that is traditionally adopted by the investment community for sustainability.

One of the most recent versions of this framework was created by the Sustainability Accounting Standards Board. It is a blend of the Five Capitals model and ESG, although it is definitely written from an organisational perspective.

For more information see:

- UN PRI's guide to ESG for Private Equity: **http://www.unpri.org/ viewer/?file=wp-content/uploads/13161_ESG_Disclosure_ Document_v6.pdf**

- Sustainability Accounting Standards Board's Universe of ESG issues: **http://www.sasb.org/wp-content/uploads/2012/03/ESG-Univ-of-Issues-2.png**

Social, Environmental & Economic (SEE)

This framework is used by DJSI to rate companies and is the basis for GRI's framework. One conception of the model appears below, although many are available.

For more information see:

- DJSI's Guidebook: http://www.sustainability-indices.com/images/ djsi-world-guidebook_tcm1071-337244.pdf

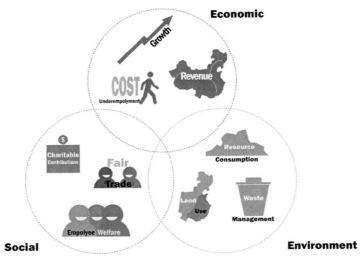

SOURCE: http://en.wikipedia.org/wiki/File:Triple_Bottom_Line_graphic.jpg

People, Planet, Profit (PPP)

This approach is often associated with Triple Bottom Line accounting, and advocates accounting for sustainability by adding ledgers for people and planet to the existing profit ledger.

For more information see:

- *The Economist*'s introduction to the Triple Bottom Line: **http://www.economist.com/node/14301663**

- John Elkington's *Cannibals with Forks*: **http://www.goodreads.com/book/show/587677.Cannibals_with_Forks**

SOURCE: http://lattitude1305.blogspot.co.uk/2010/12/lattitude-2011-3bl-people-planet-profit.html

Community, Environment, Marketplace and Workplace (CEMW)

This framework, widely used for many years by UK's Business in the Community and USA's BSR, is influential because of its widespread use predominantly in those countries, although a large number of global companies also use it. Some companies find it appealing because it categorises sustainability into four main issues that organisations seem to understand intuitively.

SOURCE: https://www.theperfumeshopjobs.com/why-us_csr.cfm

For more information see:

- Alliance Boots's use of the framework: **http://www.allianceboots. com/social-responsibilities/csr-initiatives.aspx**

TOP TIPS

✓ Pick a framework that helps your organisation see issues that
   it might otherwise miss

✓ Think outside the box

GRI's Reporting Framework

GRI's Reporting Framework is something of a default standard for
identification of sustainability issues. It's not comprehensive, and it is
something of a stretch for most companies, but it is a useful checklist of
possibly relevant issues.

A materiality process is central to the latest version of the framework
(G4); compliance requires a robust materiality process like the one
outlined in this book, although there are some additional G4-specific
parts that need to be included. The framework categorises issues into:

- Economic

- Environmental

- Human rights

- Labour practices and decent work

- Society

- Product responsibility

For more information see the GRI's Reporting portals:

- G3: **https://www.globalreporting.org/reporting/G3andG3-1/
  Pages/default.aspx**

- G4: https://www.globalreporting.org/reporting/g4/Pages/default.aspx

Gather organisational tools

Gather the organisational tools used to make decisions and review performance in your organisations, including:

- **Risk register** – often a powerful tool to drive behaviour change.

- **Value chain analysis** – which can be used to further understand connections to sustainability, particularly if it identifies supply and distribution channels.

- **SWOT/PESTEL analysis** – which will sometimes have express or implied references to sustainability issues.

- **Profit and loss report** – particularly a breakdown of all expenses by type. Some bigger expenses will be directly connected to sustainability thinking, such as resources purchased (as raw materials or manufactured goods), energy used, water used, wages paid, IP costs, legal costs, training, marketing, advertising, health and safety.

- **Management KPIs**

If those tools aren't available, or don't seem to be helpful, then you might use a simple process model in conjunction with one of the Sustainability Frameworks.

TABLE 2. Sample process model

CAPITAL	RESOURCES	INPUTS	PROCESS	OUTPUTS	END USE
Community	People	Labour	Use local staff	More skills	Stronger local communities
	Strong local community	Goodwill	Engage locally	Goodwill	Ability to grow
Environment	Metals	Parts	Assemble into units	Units	Reliability
	Energy			Logistics	GHGs
	Biodiversity			Air pollution	Recycling?
	Mining				
	Waste				
	Energy	Energy	Use energy	Energy used	GHGs
Marketplace	Local suppliers	Parts	Assemble into units	Units	Customer use (safe?)
	Good supply chain				
	Good supply chain practice	Goodwill	Maintain quality	Goodwill	Trust
					Repeat business
Workplace	Local workers	Good staff	Work	Better staff	Productivity
			Training	Healthy staff	
			Safety		

The Sample Process Model shown in Table 2 is for a small, local manufacturing operation and uses the CEMW model. It maps the chosen sustainability framework against areas of business operations, which can be a useful way to highlight areas that aren't otherwise obvious.

TIPS FOR ADVANCED COMPANIES

If your organisation already has a sophisticated understanding of sustainability, it's time to do some future gazing. Frameworks like the ones listed below will help companies to identify the sustainability issues that organisations will face from 2020 and beyond.

- BITC's Forces for Change: http://www.bitc.org.uk/our-resources/report/forces-change-global-mega-trends

- Forum for the Future's Futures programme: http://www.forumforthefuture.org/our-work/how-we-do-it/futures-diagnosis/more-about-our-futures-work

- KPMG's Expect the Unexpected: Building business value in a changing world: http://www.kpmg.com/Global/en/IssuesAndInsights/ArticlesPublications/Documents/building-business-value.pdf

- The World Business Council for Sustainable Development's Vision 2050: the new Agenda for Business: http://www.wbcsd.org/pages/edocument/edocumentdetails.aspx?id=219

- Oxford Martin Institute's Now for the long-term: http://www.oxfordmartin.ox.ac.uk/downloads/commission/Oxford_Martin_Now_for_the_Long_Term.pdf

- US National Intelligence Council's Global Trends 2030: http://publicintelligence.net/global-trends-2030/

Companies like InterFace Flor and Kingfisher are already trying to imagine how their business will need to operate in the future and are reaping rewards now as a result.

Identifying issues

The next step is to identify a long list of relevant sustainability issues. Be as specific as possible. For example, 'climate change' is a nebulous issue to attempt to address, but 'corporate CO_2 emissions' or 'increased risk from changed weather patterns/sea levels' both seem more appropriate. Consider direct operations *and* supply chains.

Sustainability Issue Record (SIR)

Using the sustainability framework you selected above, review each of the Organisational Tools you have for connections to sustainability. At this stage, simply use your understanding of the organisation and intuition about sustainability. Don't be complacent, but don't worry too much about getting absolutely every issue recorded this time around – there are plenty of opportunities to refine the list throughout the process.

Record the links in a table under the headings listed in Table 3.

TABLE 3. Sustainability Issues Record (SIR) (issues gathering)

Category	Sustainability Issue (Describe Risk/Opportunity)	Effect (Postive, Negative or Unknown)	Organisational Division	Owner (Person)	Measures Current	Targets & KPIs Current

Where possible, identify the Organisational Division that is managing the issue (or most likely to manage the issue) and include that information in the Sustainability Issues Record (SIR). Also identify measures and KPIs that currently exist or which may be useful but are not currently used. Also note the effect that the company can have on the issues (positive, negative or unclear). For some sustainability issues there may not be any information other than the issue itself to enter into the record. Enter it anyway – this is, after all, a gathering exercise.

In the first instance it will usually be useful to do this exercise by yourself or with only a few others. It is also possible to do this exercise with the Sustainability Team as a way to build rapport, however it will use significantly more resources.

Internal

Now that you have a draft SIR, refine it in conjunction with your internal stakeholders. Below are a few tips on how you might successfully do that.

Gathering information from Internal Stakeholders can use any of the usual methods like surveys, focus groups or workshops.

Current views (Sustainability Team)

Share your SIR with the Sustainability Team. If this is the first time you have done a materiality assessment, gather their thoughts about how sustainability is connected to their role and organisational unit. That could be done collectively, but in the first instance meeting individually can provide some useful insights.

If you can proceed individually, consider using the questionnaire in Appendix A. It is probably wise to listen a lot more than talk, however you may want to briefly talk them through the chosen sustainability framework and tell them which organisational tools you are using. The ten questions in the interview should take about 20–40 minutes.

If this isn't the first time you've done a materiality analysis, then send the SIR to the Sustainability Team for comment or convene a meeting to refresh the list. Ask them which stakeholders are most important to them and what the stakeholders care about. You may also want to convene special meetings with a few representatives from select organisational units.

Strategy

If you have a strategy team, convince one of them to sit down with you to review the list. Their insights into discarded strategies and access to strategic direction of your organisation should prove very useful.

Expenses (finance)

Speak with someone in finance if you are unsure what a particular category of expense means. For example, greenhouse gas emissions will be connected to energy spend, fuels purchased for energy generation and vehicle fuels (among other things). The emissions will also be present in travel which might be found in vehicle expenses, staff reimbursements and travel costs or any combination of those things.

Add to the SIR

Add any insights gathered to the SIR.

TIPS FOR ADVANCED COMPANIES – INTERNAL ANALYSIS

Companies can use a Life Cycle Analysis (LCA) to understand sustainability issues related to use of resources within the business, in the supply chain and by consumers.

A good LCA can highlight step-change efficiencies in use of resources and recycling, such as that by InterFace Flor when it changed its business model to leasing of carpets. That change meant better recyclability of all products and cheaper inputs to production.

Unilever's LCA analysis of its products and behavioural barriers to change led it to publish its 5 Levers for Change: **http://www. youtube.com/watch?v=jEaGM8kDac4**

External

External sources and stakeholders can help you identify relevant sustainability issues. There are six main sources:

- Competitors
- National legislation and soft regulation
- Industry-specific standards and frameworks
- External stakeholders
- Shareholder resolutions
- Media reviews

Competitors

Looking at your competitors helps you to benchmark your company.

Research the sustainability issues that your competitors are publicly reporting. Look at the sustainability communications of the sustainability leader in your sector (website and sustainability report are a good start). Indexes and ratings will help you to determine the leader in your sector (e.g. DJSI and FTSE4Good, among others).

Add all the issues identified by your competitors to the SIR.

You may also wish to look at lists of the most commonly reported sustainability issues that are important to stakeholders and organisations: see Appendix C – Common Material Sustainability Issues.

National legislation and soft regulation

Of course, you need to be aware of national legislation and soft regulation (e.g. accounting standards, stock market listing rules, local expectations); they are an important source of sustainability issues.

Industry-specific standards and frameworks

GRI and SASB have identified material issues for organisations in some sectors:

- GRI's sector supplements: **https://www.globalreporting.org/ reporting/sectorguidance/sector-guidance/Pages/default.aspx**

- SASB's sector guides: **http://www.sasb.org/**

SASB's approach uses a limited set of sustainability issues and is backward looking because it is evidence-based, but can be a good beginning point. Increasingly stakeholders will see sector-specific frameworks as a minimum standard of compliance.

Check for any other sector-specific frameworks with industry groups relevant to your organisation. A relatively comprehensive list of sector-specific sustainability reporting frameworks has been collected by Corporate Sustainability Reporting: **http://www.reportingcsr.org/_extractive_industries-p-163.html**

You will still need to make decisions about whether each issue applies to your organisation. For example, the EITI has been criticised because it identified issues relevant to the largest extractors, and not for smaller and support companies in the sector.

Add any further issues identified to the SIR.

External stakeholders

> *Really pay attention to negative feedback and solicit it, particularly from friends . . . Hardly anyone does that, and it's incredibly helpful.*
>
> ELON MUSK, CEO TESLA MOTORS, FEBRUARY 2013[3]

Stakeholders have recently become more important in the corporate world, especially in relation to sustainability reporting because they identify relevant sustainability issues. More radical stakeholders often give clues as to the issues of tomorrow. Including their views is vital to building a useful materiality analysis that is ready for future cycles. Of course, the voices of stakeholders are highly subjective, and there is the risk of being blown from social issue to social issue.

From your list of influential external stakeholders, identify the ones that you think will provide the most useful insights of your organisation. Ask them what they think are the most important sustainability issues for your organisation.

To engage stakeholders, you could use:

- Roundtables

- Surveys

- Interviews

- Guest attendance at a meeting of your Sustainability Team

- Online forums

- Phone conferences

- Supplier conventions

- Stakeholder collaborations

A form of materiality process *could* be completed without the input of external stakeholders, but any conclusions drawn will be unreliable. Credibility, accuracy and reliability of outcomes are all significantly increased by the direct input of external stakeholders.

Shareholder resolutions

With the number of shareholder resolutions on the rise, smart sustainability professionals will grab the report on the last shareholder proxy season. The quality of research on shareholder proxies is probably best in the US, but other research can be found.

Review all the issues identified and make note of any that may be relevant for your organisation.

Media reviews

Media reviews (including traditional news sources, search engines and social media) can reveal some really interesting sustainability issues, but they can also reveal a lot of noise. Targeted media reviews that search with sector-specific terms can be a valuable source of issues.

TIPS FOR ADVANCED COMPANIES

Companies that are very sophisticated at Scanning will develop scenario plans that include best and worst case scenarios for the adoption of sustainability. Such a process needs the input of an organisation's business planners and should incorporate the views of external experts on sustainability.

Transparency of assumptions and logical connections are the backbone of any Scenario Planning, which will enable the organisation to make plans for various outcomes.

PRIORITISE

[There are ...] more than 500 sustainability issues ... currently tracked by dozens of entities, relying on more than 2,000 indicators.[4]

Deciding which issues are most relevant is probably the most difficult part of completing a materiality process. It is fraught with political danger because if done well it will necessarily provoke change within your organisation, which could also involve new targets, reporting lines and responsibilities. Discussions about relevance of issues can feel uncomfortable because they involve talking about things on which the organisation is not necessarily expert, and involve a rather diverse range of participants that don't often work together. But it can yield impressive results!

Consolidate and clarify

At this stage you should consolidate the list of sustainability issues, merging any that are similar, while ensuring that you preserve clarity and differences where they exist. You should also check that the list doesn't have generic terms like 'health and safety' or 'diversity'.

Issues should be specific, but still reflect the organisation-wide process and impact of the organisation on the issue (and its supply chain if that is within your contemplation).

Which issues?

Organisations will take a variety of approaches to accepting or rejecting responsibility for their impacts outside their direct operations. Broadly speaking, the approaches fall into three categories:

- **Minimalist legal** – Responsibility is limited to only the things for which the organisation is directly responsible and for which it can be legally held accountable.

- **Control** – Responsibility is accepted for impacts extending into contractual relationships and for end-use. Typically that involves working directly with suppliers and consumer groups.

- **Holistic** – Mechanisms of value creation (or destruction) wherever they occur are included. That is, the organisation is interested in any impact that creates or destroys value anywhere in the supply chain or at the end of a service or product's life.

There is a loose correlation between sustainability maturity and the chosen boundary – sustainability maturity usually means increasingly holistic approaches and the use of tools like life-cycle analysis and footprint identification. However, most organisations set different boundaries for respective issues, based on relevance of the issue.

It seems useful to determine relevance of issues before making decisions about which approach is relevant. Organisations that do so are able to decide which issues require a holistic approach (because of the importance to the organisation) and which issues can safely be dealt with using a more minimalist approach. Even some of the leaders in sustainability have areas where they are still primarily focused on a minimalist legal approach.

Both GRI and IIRC reporting frameworks have requirements in relation to boundaries so, if they are relevant for you, then it's worth reviewing their respective requirements at this stage.

Importance to stakeholders

Next you need to determine the importance of each issue to stakeholders, both identifiable stakeholders and voiceless stakeholders (such as the six capitals or the environment). Add another column at the end of the SIR, titled 'Importance to Stakeholders'.

Allocate a score (1–10) for the importance of each issue to stakeholders. This will be something of a fudged number unless there has been a thorough stakeholder engagement process, and even then the number will remain somewhat intuitive and represent a compromise of the rating of importance of stakeholders from different organisational units.

Organisations often begin with stakeholders they are already close to, and give priority to seeking their views. That is a sensible approach, so long as over time all stakeholders are appropriately identified and their views included. After all, when it comes to stakeholders, unless there is direct dialogue, you can never be sure you understand their concerns.

There is also a tension between the variety of stakeholders that may have an opinion on any give issue. It may be worthwhile prioritising stakeholders on issues and giving increased ranking to more important ones for that particular issue.

There are many more sophisticated ways to allocate a score to the Importance to stakeholders, but no consensus on this.

FIGURE 9. SAP's external stakeholder issues.

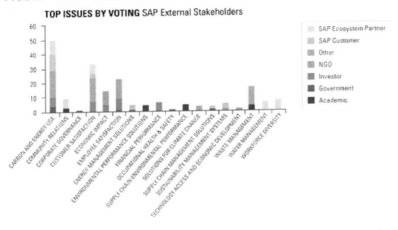

TOP ISSUES BY VOTING SAP External Stakeholders

In sharpening your intuition about which number to use, it can be useful to track the number of stakeholders who think an issue is important, as in Figure 9. However, the number of stakeholders mentioning an issue may not be decisive nor an appropriate way to allocate a value to importance to stakeholders. In some circumstances, one stakeholder's views will be enough to make the issue very important, while in other circumstances several stakeholders might mention an issue, but it won't rank very highly.

Try to get the number right, but don't stop the process here because it is difficult. Make your best estimate and move on. There is plenty more work to do and in any case you will need to gather some consensus on the relative importance of stakeholder views!

TIPS FOR ADVANCED COMPANIES

Companies with a thorough stakeholder engagement process may want to use two or more metrics to calculate an 'Importance to Stakeholders' number; using a number for Stakeholder Rating and another number for Extent of Issue or Influence. The formula looks something the one below.

Of course, this score is still rather intuitive, and the importance of social media shouldn't be underestimated, but a two metric approach can provide insights that a single-metric score may not make obvious.

$$\frac{\textbf{Stakeholder Rating x Extent of Issue or Influence}}{\textbf{Maximum Scale Score}}$$

$$= \textbf{Importance to Stakeholders}$$

Additional metrics to consider include:

- Stakeholder Expectations of action on the issue and

- Potential for disruption or negative press/campaigns.

The latter is fraught with some danger in that the most damaging campaigns are often the ones that seem completely unpredictable.

Importance to organisation

In calculating a score for importance to organisation, you must understand the culture of your organisation. If your organisation is driven by risk and compliance issues, then a purely risk approach is an excellent place to start. If your organisation is driven by sales and new markets then a purely opportunity approach might be useful.

In any case the framework below gives a degree of flexibility. Understanding the focus of your organisation may mean that you use only certain metrics, or add only those relevant to your context. Hopefully you have already spoken to several internal stakeholders and have a sense of how to appeal to them.

If your organisation uses other tools for assessing risk, then consider integrating those tools with the method proposed below, or simply use those tools instead.

Risk/opportunity and materiality

To calculate the importance to organisation score, you should use a typical risk/opportunity framework. Doing so involves assessing the impact of an event and the likelihood of the event occurring.

For example, it's not very likely that a hurricane will appear off the UK coast and then destroy Brighton. But if it did, the impact would be catastrophic for Brighton residents, and any warehouse you might have there. That's an example from the risk perspective, but the same type of analysis applies to opportunities.

Add three columns to the end of the SIR, as shown in Table 4 (with the first four columns of the Sustainability Issues Record not shown).

For the purposes of the SIR, risk and opportunity are two sides of the same coin. Virtually all risks can be re-described as opportunities and vice versa, but because companies will have different cultures of risk and opportunity, it is good to leave the framework somewhat ambiguous.

You can also draw on the experience and skills of the risk management team; a Director's view will be especially useful.

....

TABLE 4. Sustainability Issues Record (showing impacts)

Measures	Targets & KPIs	Importance to Stakeholders	Importance to Organisation (Risk / Opportunity)		
Current	Current	Score	Impact	Likelihood	Score

....

Impact

Impact refers to the consequences to the organisation of an event occurring. For organisations familiar with a risk analysis, they will often have a series of categories of damage resulting from a risk. If the relevant scale of impact is 1–10, then 1 might be up to £500, while 10 might be greater than £50,000,000 as in Table 5.

Use the same framework to calculate the size of the opportunity. If there is both risk and opportunity, add the score for risk to the score for opportunity.

Of course, it can be difficult to know just how much impact an issue can have, and therefore difficult to allocate a score. Make a best guess (keeping in mind the accounting principle of conservatism) and flag the issue for discussion in the Sense Check phase (below).

TABLE 5. Sample impact score

SCORE	DESCRIPTION	£ RANGE
1	Negligible	0–£499
2	Minor	£200–£2,499
3	Significant	£1,000–£9,999
4	Very Significant	£5,000–£49,999
5	Moderate	£20,000–£99,999
6	Moderately large	£100,000–£399,999
7	Large	£400,000–£1,999,999
8	Very Large	£2,000,000–£9,999,999
9	Huge	£10,000,000–£49,999,999
10	Catastrophic!	£50,000,000 +

NOTE: these figures are not a recommendation, merely a guide to categories of impact.

There is nothing magic about having a 1–10 scale and a five-point scale can also work well, however longer scales give better differentiation of the issues in later processes. Align the SIR to whatever scales your organisation uses and ensure that you adjust any mathematical formulas accordingly. A 2 x 2 matrix might be useful when publishing a limited set of information, but it is totally inadequate in an internal context.

Likelihood

Likelihood refers to the chances of a particular event occurring. In the Brighton hurricane example, it is probably less than 1,000,000 to 1 in any given year, based on historical models. Looking up those odds in Table 6 it would merit a score of 1. The Brighton hurricane isn't likely if you use historical models, but the more appropriate model is one that incorporates the effect of climate change on the UK's weather patterns. If the chances of a hurricane forming and destroying Brighton are now 1000 to 1, it would rate 3 on the same scale. Presumably, the impact score would not change.

Usually organisations use their business planning timeline to calculate a score. If that timeline is quite short, for example, three years or less, then many longer-terms risks will be ignored. Even a 100 to 1 hurricane event wouldn't rate very highly with a three-year timeline (with odds of 33 to 1) and merit a score of 5. But with a 25-year timescale, the odds drop significantly to 4 to 1, which is a very significant level of likelihood and would merit 7 on the scale.

TABLE 6. Sample likelihood scoring

SCORE	DESCRIPTION	ODDS
1	Almost never going to happen	> 12,500-1
2	Almost certain to not happen this cycle	12,500-1
3	Extremely unlikely to happen this cycle	2,500-1
4	Very unlikely to happen this cycle	500-1
5	Unlikely to happen in this cycle	100-1
6	Not likely to happen this cycle	20-1
7	Might happen this cycle	4-1
8	Likely to happen this cycle	2-1
9	Almost certain to happen this cycle	1-1
10	Likely to happen multiple times this cycle	< 1-1

NOTE: these figures are not a recommendation, merely a guide to categories of likelihood.

Risk/opportunity score

By multiplying likelihood and impact scores for a particular issue, an overall risk/opportunity score is identified. Because two scores have been multiplied, they need to be reduced to match the level of the importance to stakeholders (in this case 1–10). In our example the score needs to be divided by 10. That score can be used for the 'importance to business' metric.

$$\frac{\text{Impact x Likelihood}}{\text{Maximum Scale Score}} = \text{Importance to Business}$$

Other metrics

In addition to simple impact and likelihood scores, there are also a raft of additions that can simply be 'bolted on' to the Sustainability Issues Record and subsequent calculation. If additional metrics are used, then a further equalisation will need to occur to ensure the derived number is comparable to the number for importance to stakeholders.

Examples of other metrics that may be useful are:

- **Long term**: Adding a time dimension is useful if companies have become addicted to very short time-lines on sustainability issues. The initial score may be for usual business timescales and the additional score reflect variation if a longer timescale is used.

- **Net effect on Natural Capitals**: Calculating figures in such a way as to be reliable can be tricky, but may give useful insight.

- **Influence of stakeholder**: Understanding how much influence stakeholders can have is a dangerous, but at times valid assessment to make.

- **Collaboration Forces:** Understanding how much impetus there is for collaboration can be useful.

- **Ability to Mitigate:** Understanding a companies ability or otherwise to reduce certain risks may effect decision-making.

TOP TIPS

✓ Don't get too bogged down in trying to find the next big sustainability time-bomb.

✓ Keep the focus on the impacts of the things that can be controlled and mitigated.

TIPS FOR ADVANCED COMPANIES

Adding qualitative descriptions for the categories of risk/opportunity can add value to this task.

Some organisations also have different categories of risk/opportunity for different areas of sustainability which are difficult to accurately quantify. For example, if employee turnover is a relevant risk, an organisation might use percentage categories in order to quantify risks. A rating of 1 might be <3% turnover while a 10 might be >15% turnover.

Materiality matrix

After you have identified the importance of each issue to stakeholders and the organisation, compile a materiality matrix, using the importance to stakeholders score and importance to organisation score. If the list of relevant issues is quite long, then you may want to map only the top 30 or so issues.

FIGURE 10. Kesko's 2012 materiality matrix.

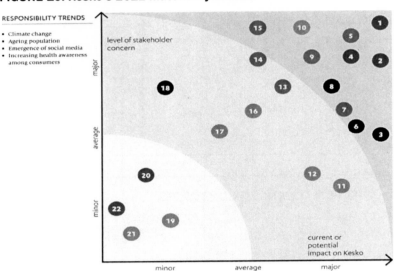

RESPONSIBILITY TRENDS

- Climate change
- Ageing population
- Emergence of social media
- Increasing health awareness among consumers

level of stakeholder concern

major

average

minor

current or potential impact on Kesko

minor   average   major

HUMAN RESOURCES RESPONSIBILITY

- ❸ Development of personnel competences and versatile jobs
- ❻ Occupational health and safety
- ❹ Good working community (fair, provides equal opportunities and promotes employee wellbeing)
- ❿ Steady employment

RESPONSIBLE PURCHASING AND SALES

- ❽ Product safety
- ❷ Responsible marketing and sales, and responsibility communications
- ❾ Promotion of healthy lifestyles
- ⑫ Shopping safety
- ⑭ Origin of products, purchasing policy definitions, and working conditions and human rights throughout the purchasing chain
- ⑮ Product selection (local suppliers, pro-environmental products and services, organic, Fairtrade)

ECONOMIC RESPONSIBILITY

- ❶ Profitability of operations
- ❺ Good corporate governance and risk management
- ❹ Comprehensiveness and accessibility of store network and electronic services
- ⑳ Impact on regional business activities
- ㉒ Support to non-profit operations

ENVIRONMENTAL RESPONSIBILITY

- ⑯ Energy efficiency in store operations, products and services
- ⑪ Efficient logistics
- ⑬ Optimisation of packaging
- ⑯ Environmental management of stores and advice to customers
- ⑰ Environmental impacts from production in the purchasing chain
- ⑱ Water consumption in real estate properties
- ㉑ Promotion of sustainable agriculture

What it is

A materiality matrix is a visual representation of the sustainability issues relevant to your organisation. When done well, it can aid speed of understanding and comprehension of sustainability issues and relative materiality. An example of a materiality matrix is that of Kesko, a Finnish retail and wholesale conglomerate, in Figure 10.

When done badly (or if it is integrated back in into the business badly) it can marginalise sustainability or be seen as a burdening cost on the organisation with little value. See below for some top tips on making a materiality matrix work.

How to do it

Graph the SIR issues using importance to stakeholders on one axis and importance to organisation on the other.

Variations

Additional information can be plotted on a materiality matrix using colour, size of point marker and other labelling to communicate additional information. That means that there are at least five types of information that can be communicated on a materiality matrix.

Other categories of information which might be useful are:

- Categorisation of sustainability issues by type
- Number of stakeholders concerned about the issue
- Competitive aspects, including how well direct competition is dealing with the issue
- Trend lines, in relation to past or intended future performance

- Business expenditure in relation to the issue

- Current performance compared to future performance (perhaps represented by size of the indicator)

If any of those dimensions are going to be used, then gathering relevant data obviously needs to happen throughout the materiality process.

It is also possible to produce something of a hybrid materiality matrix which will satisfy both GRI and IIRC versions of the materiality process. Although it isn't conclusive, the model put forward by BSR (Figure 11) shows one way to blend the two approaches. The axis which would be

FIGURE 11. BSR's hybrid materiality matrix.

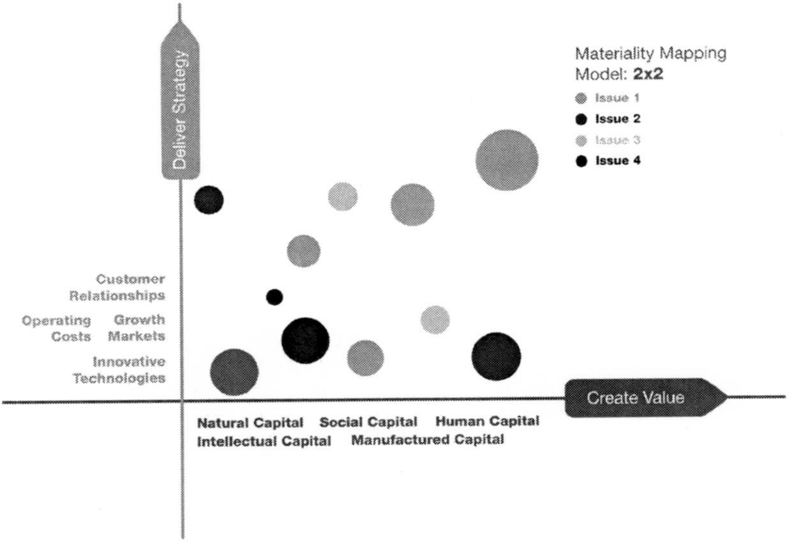

SOURCE: http://www.greenbiz.com/blog/2013/08/20/navigating-materiality

'importance to stakeholders' is replaced with 'create value' and the 'importance to business' is replaced with 'deliver strategy'.

The blended approach above removes the intuitive assessment of relative importance of stakeholders, but in many ways creates as many problems as it solves. It places all capitals on the same plane, which is hardly ideal (and similar to the dilemma of prioritising stakeholders). That's a big problem because there isn't any consensus on how to account for the capitals in a way that would lead to a reliable calculation. It also increases complexity within any kind of calculation of a single score to represent such diverse value-creation/destruction capitals. But it also solves problems that may otherwise arise because of aligning compliance to GRI and IIRC frameworks.

Other types of graphs are also possible, especially given the multiple layers of information that are important in a materiality context. Variations on spider diagrams can be expected to emerge in the coming years, although the effort required to 'decode' such diagrams seems exponentially greater than a simple two-axis graph.

Visualising

The rise in popularity of 'infographics' shows that data visualisation doesn't have to be boring. Recent versions of the materiality matrix (such as Figures 12 and 13) also show that a materiality matrix can be beautiful too. OK, that may be going too far, but a commitment to the materiality matrix as a visual communication tool will reap rewards. People who care about sustainability can access a lot of information in a short period of time and in doing so can create trust.

. . . .

FIGURE 12. International Flavours and Fragrances' materiality matrix.

MATERIALITY MATRIX

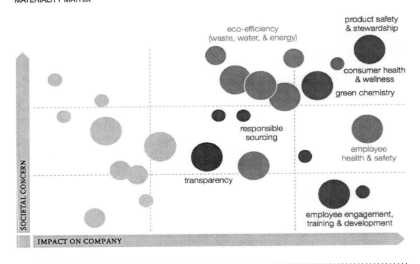

. . . .

Because of the nature of numbers, and depending on your organisational profile, you may need to do some tricky things with the graphs, like using logarithmic instead of linear scales (you do have someone from finance on your Sustainability Team, don't you?).

FIGURE 13. State Street's materiality matrix.

TIPS FOR ADVANCED COMPANIES

- Companies that get the most value from their Matrix do several things to avoid letting the Matrix be a dead-end tool.

- Do it in 3D, 4D or even 5D. Some of the best use 3 or 4 layers of information, using colour, size and background identification to add meaning

- Issues in the Matrix have KPIs and targets, which are reported clearly and connected to the materiality process

- Circulate it widely across the organisation – it is an excellent conversational tool

- Produce bespoke versions for specific target audiences, which can highlight how issues can create or destroy organisational value in ways that are relevant to certain groups

- Send a copy to people who contributed to its development. It's remarkable how positively people can respond if they feel part of something bigger

- Focus on the issues most important to stakeholders and the business and don't get lost in the minor issues

- Measure and manage the most important issues and periodically remind the organisation (subtly of course) of the value of the Materiality process

- Communicate on the issues that need 'fixing' and be clear about why the other issues aren't being addressed at the present time

- Ensure that people understand the matrix as a mid-point in a process and not a final output

Sense check

After the prioritisation process has concluded, then the relevance of sustainability issues should be sense-checked within the organisation. Use the materiality matrix and also the Sustainability Issues Record for that process.

As you are sharing the information back, focus on communicating the information and on cementing the relationships that you have already established.

Internal

Some of the most successful interventions I have been involved with have gathered the Sustainability Team (and Special Advisers) to discuss and agree on importance to the stakeholder and the organisation. That requires a significant amount of resource (mostly time) and often two or three meetings to traverse all the issues. That commitment can result in a degree of consensus that can be really useful for other parts of the process.

TOP TIPS FOR A CONSENSUS PROCESS

- Schedule more than one session to talk
- Give people space to express opinions
- *Listen lots*
- Tell them you are aiming for a sensible outsider's perspective
- Ask questions
- Let people differ and encourage dialogue

If you can't gather the full team to build consensus, you could make initial assessments about the issues and meet to workshop differences with the Sustainability Team. Alternatively discuss with the Team on an individual basis or send it to them inviting feedback. Because consensus is so important to the next steps, a meeting of the Sustainability Team seems essential at this point.

As part of the process it can be useful to communicate how you got to where you are and the tools that you have used along the way. Explain you are trying to get a picture of the company that is sensible to insiders and helps outsiders understand where the company is at.

Take notes and keep quiet where possible. Avoid the temptation to justify any particular decision or score and listen to their perspectives.

External

There is also often value to having some external validation of the sustainability issues that the company has concluded are most important.

Proxies for a wide range of stakeholders can be very useful at this point and can help to identify new issues, clarify likely direction of travel on emerging issues, identify missing stakeholders and give an outsider's perspective.

After you have met with external stakeholders, share their perspective with the team that formed the priorities and sense-check conclusions with them.

Material Sustainability Issues (MSIs)

If this is your first time at a materiality process, pick the top five to fifteen issues to target. Usually they would be the most relevant issues as shown in the top right of your materiality matrix (although there can be organisational reasons to not pick the most material, such as a strategic review or other operational or political reasons).

Make a list of your new Material Sustainability Issues (MSIs) and book yourself a reservation at your favourite restaurant to congratulate yourself.

Lay aside the rest of the sustainability issues until next year, when you can target management of several more.

EMBED

Materiality is seen as an outcome rather than a process ... the true value of materiality is still not widely understood or appreciated[5]

Materiality only really gains any significant influence over business performance when the noise and clutter of the many thousands of sustainability issues have been quieted to a few remaining and relevant MSIs. Understanding that the MSIs are representative of issues that can create or destroy significant amounts of value is an important step in embedding them into the organisation.

Companies have been 'doing' materiality for many years, including producing materiality matrices. That's good, because it means there are several kinds of materiality matrices around to inspire your process. But it doesn't mean that the issues identified are fully integrated into the core of all of those organisations.

Change process

A few organisations that I approached about being a case study for this book declined because, while they publish a materiality matrix each year, they hadn't been able to fully embed their external processes within the organisation. Embedding your MSIs into the organisation won't be easy.

Incorporating sustainability issues (even the most relevant ones) involves a complex series of mechanics that are well beyond the scope of this book. However, it is important to recognise that the embedding process involves the culture of the organisation, its leadership, internal communications and various engagement processes. This brief guide to embedding will offer some materiality-specific insights to help connect sustainability to business as usual.

Embedding the MSIs will mean measurement of new metrics and/ or using existing metrics in new ways. It will also mean subtle (if not profound) changes of strategic direction and having people take on new responsibilities.

You might also find help from another guide in this series:

- *Green Jujitsu: The Smart Way to Embed Sustainability into Your Organisation*

Gap analysis

Once the MSIs are clear, review the Sustainability Issues Record and identify gaps in terms of organisational division, owner, measures and KPIs. A complete gap analysis is useful because achieving positive results on MSIs can be supported by fixing gaps in other issues.

For example, say you are a professional services firm and staff retention is a big issue for you (and one of your MSIs). Scores on your Employee Engagement Survey is one of your KPIs, along with staff turnover. Employee volunteering in local community initiatives is on the SIR, and you suspect that employees that volunteer are happier, healthier and generally a bit better than those who don't. In that case, it's probably sensible also to track volunteerism against performance ratings, staff retention and Employee Engagement scores as part of the employee retention figures for the relevant MSI.

There is a bit of intuition and opportunism required here, so be on the lookout for opportunities to move the dial on multiple MSIs. The

Sustainability Team are able to help and they may have needs that you can help meet. You may be able to get some traction by showing the very long list of sustainability issues identified (SIR) compared to the quite short MSI and asking where they see synergy.

If you are having trouble convincing the organisation that issues are relevant, you may wish to do some benchmarking and report on what your competitors are doing. It can be very powerful to show that all competitors are reporting on one of your MSIs and your organisation is not. No-one really likes to be last in league tables (so if you are, be careful how you present this information).

Ownership

Finding a sensible owner for each of the issues won't always be easy, although they often identify themselves (or can be identified by the Sustainability Team) as issues are discussed throughout the process. If they don't, then you will need to use your powers of persuasion or the leverage of high-ranking supporters of sustainability to find a suitable owner. The character of your organisation is important here. Top-down cultures will probably want decisions to come from above, while flatter organisations will want to reach agreement. Either way, your new analysis of risk and opportunity of the sustainability issue will be important as a convincing tool.

Your task of encouraging ownership will be easier if there is an organisational division that will benefit (financially or in some other way) from owning the MSI or be harmed if it isn't handled well (you may also need to build a business case for the particular issue). Studies that highlight how other organisations have solved the issue will help. Very few of you will be looking at issues that have not been successfully dealt with before.

Stakeholder relationships should be owned by the organisational division with the most contact with that stakeholder. As a last resort, take ownership yourself, but be very slow to reach that conclusion unless the Sustainability Team reaps significant benefit from doing so. Usually you don't have either the leverage or the relationships to make that a cost-effective decision.

You don't have enough resources to tackle all of the gaps at the same time. You may not even have enough resources to do a great job of more than a few things. Do a really good job of a few of the MSIs and resign yourself to making progress more slowly on others.

Integrate MSIs into the risk register

Where possible, all of the MSIs should be included in the relevant risk register, along with details of the owner of the risk and details of steps being taken to mitigate risks (or maximise opportunities).

Doing so will give visibility to sustainability issues at board level and help people outside the Sustainability Team know that sustainability issues are being managed. It will also help with the next steps of embedding sustainability issues.

Before attempting to get MSIs entered on the risk register it is important to understand that the risk team might understand the term 'materiality' quite differently to members of the sustainability profession (for more details on that see above).

It is also useful to understand that risk registers can accommodate different internal perspectives on the same issue, although it won't always be the case that risk managers will record such risks separately. For example, the risk that the organisation won't meet increasing demands included in pre-qualification processes may impact organisational units quite differently and it may be useful to record the separately identifiable risk levels in the risk register.

Equally some risks are more sensibly aggregated because only in aggregate do risks become significant. Climate change effects are probably an example of issues that will appear much large and riskier if considered in aggregate.

Measurement

Create a list of all the things on the gap analysis that you would like to be able to measure that aren't currently measured. When making that list, it might be useful to have two thought processes:

- *How much could we benefit (cost savings and increased revenue)?*

- *How much is it costing us now (legacy costs)?*

For example, in order to show improvement in retaining talent, there needs to be a benchmark of current performance, and the organisation may need to spend some time calculating how much turnover currently costs. That would include time spent recruiting (by line managers, HR and others involved in the process), advertising costs, sacrifices in productivity during orientation periods, training costs, recruiters fees and other related expenses.

Identifying legacy costs and using them as a benchmark of future performance is especially useful if there is scepticism in parts of the organisation that sustainability can add to the bottom line. In those circumstances it can be very important to measure costs *before* making a change. It's very difficult to reverse-engineer previous costs after making a change, and besides that people forget very quickly about why the change was made.

Of course, while gathering all this information you have constant opportunities to be talking to all kinds of people about sustainability and the benefits that it brings. Use those opportunities wisely and don't forget to listen.

Targets and KPIs

Note current targets and KPIs in the SIR, and brainstorm some targets that might change behaviour and create value in the business. Targets will need to be set in conjunction with the issue owner and agreed by the Sustainability Team.

You may need to also add performance targets to people's review processes in order to encourage behaviour change. For example, if your organisation wants to encourage use of more sustainability-focused suppliers, you probably won't achieve it if procurement staff are given a bonus only for achieving price reductions. They need other bonus targets that directly relate to sustainability.

Targets can be performance numbers and also qualitative descriptions, or both. For example, it might be a target to put in place a sustainable procurement policy and have 50% of suppliers comply. The policy is a qualitative target and the 50% is a performance target.

Remember too that Marks & Spencer (see Case Study) didn't have any benchmark, comparator or pioneers who had forged the way before they set down plans to spend £40m annually on sustainability. Their boldness with targets and KPIs has paid off, with a greater than 60% annual ROI on sustainability as of 2013.

Prioritise and plan

Look at the list of gaps that you have now created. Rank them in some kind of priority, being guided by their position on the materiality matrix and your intuition and knowledge of the organisation.

Oh yes, and start locking away dates in next year's diary for a repeat of the process you have just been through.

CASE STUDY: SAP

SAP and Sustainability

SAP's public commitment to sustainability started in 2007 when the company generated its first sustainability report. Its stated approach to sustainability is to 'holistically manage social, environmental and economic risks and opportunities for enhanced profitability, reputation and compliance'.

SAP believes that the private sector plays a vital role in creating a level playing field, driving innovation and building an environment that enhances education and entrepreneurship to foster economic growth while taking social and environmental responsibility.

SAP strives to have an 'exemplar' strategy, while leading the market as 'enabler' with sustainability solutions. In 2013, SAP published its first integrated report.

SAP's approach to materiality

SAP sees materiality as a fundamental principle of a sustainable strategy, along with integrated reporting. Disclosure of its materiality assessment is important to investors, companies, regulators and the public for many reasons. Regulators already require certain disclosures and institutional investors today consider various aspects of sustainability, but more and more stakeholders are interested in additional information.

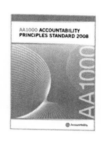

SAP has repeatedly refined its materiality assessment over the past several years. It engages in ongoing dialog with internal and external stakeholders, and follows the principles of inclusivity and responsiveness, as defined in the AA1000 AccountAbility Principles Standard (2008).

Its prioritization of materiality issues is a direct outcome of ongoing stakeholder dialogs, strategy reviews, and analysis of technology megatrends. In order to manage each such issue, SAP:

- shifted towards integrated reporting (rather than isolated sustainability reporting) to create a corporate and sustainability strategies;

- does not distinguish stakeholder issues from company material issues any longer, instead focusing on a consolidated list of material issues; and

- incorporated a broader sustainability view across all Capitals (SAP's capitals are a bespoke version of the **Capitals models** outlined on page 51), as follows:

  - **Human capital management** – (see Capitals models)
  - **Intellectual capital management** – (see Capitals models)
  - **Security and privacy** – design and deliver our solutions with the very highest levels of data security and privacy control
  - **Business conduct** – upholding the highest levels of ethical behaviour, as set out in its Code of Business Conduct and other company policies
  - **Climate and energy** – reduce and minimize the environmental impact of our solutions and corporate operations.

As 'enabler' of sustainability solutions for others, SAP also seeks growth opportunities across all 5 of its strategic pillars:

- **Applications** – Bringing sustainability performance capability to the backbone of companies via software

- **Analytics** – Exploring connections between data sets (for example, impact of energy consumption and energy cost on operating profit) and offering new approaches

- **Cloud** – Enabling easier access so more companies can use our software for their sustainable success

- **Database and Technology** – Helping solve issues related to Big Data, and delivering information in real time

- **Mobile** – Helping provide business opportunities to those often excluded by markets and accelerating processes and decisions with real time and mobile information

SAP's materiality processes have helped it identify opportunities in sustainability.

Lessons from Early Days

In 2007 SAP published its sustainability report to respond to questions from investors, credit-rating firms, business partners and other stakeholders about its environmental, human, and social metrics. But from the beginning it also had its focus on questions that were relevant to its own bottom line and the long term success

FIGURE CS2.1 – SAP's Stakeholders Top Material Issues

TOP ISSUES BY VOTING SAP External Stakeholders

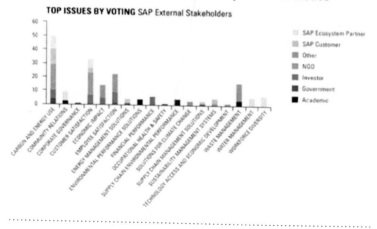

of the company, such as calculating employee turnover, staff diversity, and customer satisfaction.

SAP's materiality definition changed when instead of using their own views on stakeholders they included them in the materiality dialogue in the belief that 'direct conversation creates trust and avoids surprises'. It also includes seeking challenging stakeholders that represent issues of voiceless stakeholders (such as the environment). Figure CS2.1 (above) shows the resulting issues list after including external stakeholders in the process.

SAP's material issues

Table CS2.1 shows how sustainability issues identified from its stakeholder dialogue are categorised at a high level and the areas of business KPIs, many of which are a direct result of its materiality process.

TABLE CS2.1 – SAP's Material Issues

OBJECTIVE	CATEGORY	SUB-CATEGORY
Financial	Revenue and Income	• Liquidity and Cashflow • Assets and Equity • Expenses
	Operating Margin	
	Customer Success	
Environmental	Carbon emissions and Energy	• GHG footprint • Energy Consumed • Data Centre Energy • Renewable Energy

OBJECTIVE	CATEGORY	SUB-CATEGORY
Social	Employee Engagement and retention	
	Business Health Culture Index	
	Women in Management	
	Social Investment	• Volunteer hours • Technology donations • Capital invested • Lives impacted
	Capacity Building	
	Ranking	

SAP's materiality process is directly connected to many areas of the business:

- External reporting
- Governance
- Strategy setting
- Board reporting
- KPI setting processes

The decision to include the results of the materiality process in an integrated report allowed it to think differently about internal modelling of value creation and helped to directly connect to strategy and governance.

In challenging itself to go beyond assumptions, and by starting

FIGURE CS2.2 – SAP's Financial and Non-financial Connections Model

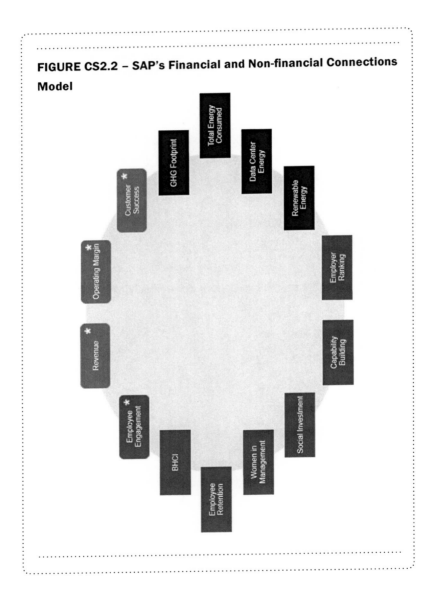

to publish calculated business value, SAP is able to correlate materiality indicators in organisational diagrams (Figure CS2.2).

Two examples of the correlations will illustrate how sustainability issues have been connected to its business.

Firstly, the environmental indicator 'GHG Footprint' (sum of all greenhouse gas emissions measured and reported, including renewable energy and 3rd party reductions) has measureable connections to the indicators shown in Figure CS2.3, namely Business Health Culture Index, Employer Ranking, Employee Engagement, Revenue and Customer Success.

FIGURE CS2.3 – 'GHG Footprint' Connections

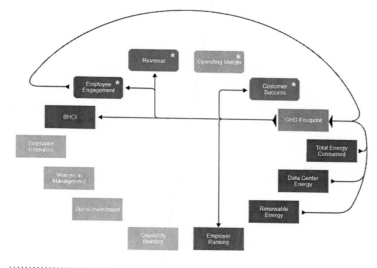

Lowering SAP's carbon emissions has a positive reputational effect, thereby enhancing SAP's standing with its customers and employees. SAP has measured increased carbon efficiency resulting in cost savings of €235 million since 2008 (compared to a "business as usual" 2007 baseline).

FIGURE CS2.4 – 'Employee Retention' Connections

Secondly, as shown in Figure CS2.4, SAP found that the social indicator 'Employee Retention' has connections to:

- Capability Building
- Business Health Culture Index
- Employee Engagement

- Revenue
- Customer Success (akin to customer satisfaction)
- Operating Margin

One result showed that a 1% turnover per year will typically lead to more than €62 million impact on operating result.

Over time, SAP plans to intensify its internal studies on how material sustainability indicators affect SAP's financial performance.

The materiality process outlined above is a journey requiring ongoing re-evaluation and questioning, and SAP is still learning.

For more information about SAP integrated reporting and materiality journey, please visit: http://www.sapintegratedreport.com/2012/en/key-facts/connecting-financial-and-non-financial-performance.html

Co-written by the author and Thomas Odenwald, Senior Vice President, SAP.

MANAGE

You can't manage what you don't measure.[6]

If you have successfully embedded all the MSIs through targets, KPIs, ownership and inspiration, then you still have work to do. Management tips are limited in this publication to some of the most pressing things flowing from a materiality process.

Integrating into business as usual

The Scan and Prioritisation steps of the process are distinctly outside usual organisational processes. That's because external stakeholders are engaged, but it's important to integrate the conclusions of the process into normal organisational processes.

Your goal now is to align sustainability issues with regular management processes. Figure 14 shows how the process in this book can conceptually be connected to usual business process.

While some linkages will be intuitive and obvious, some will require some effort to ensure that they are achieved. Doing so involves:

- Sustainability information being available in time for other organisational processes. For example, if the board currently gets quarterly reports on the health of the organisation, then performance against sustainability goals are updated quarterly.

- Other people having access to sustainability data as and when they need it. That probably means ensuring alignment or transportability between IT systems (or giving others access to your growing tranche of spreadsheets).

FIGURE 14. Materiality process – integrating into business.[7]

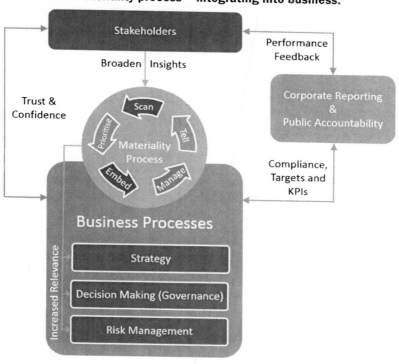

- Giving others ownership of and responsibility for sustainability targets.

You should also investigate whether there is appetite to have discussions with senior management about the ways sustainability is indicating emerging issues and new business opportunities.

Quick wins and the first 100 days

Keep an eye on which of the MSIs will give you 'quick wins' or success in the first 100 days after Prioritisation. The action plan should include:

- how you will communicate success back into the organisation

- which communications channels are relevant (including the Sustainability Team)

- how sustainability issues are helping make the organisation better (presumably through decreased risk or increased opportunities)

- how stakeholder engagement has helped build success

- how the identified success is part of something bigger.

You don't need to go from nothing to Plan A in one leap. You just need to get started, and be open to let the next steps follow. From such humble beginnings, great achievements can be made.[8]

Owner maintenance

Periodically check in with owners of MSIs to see how they are doing at managing their issues. Ensure that they understand what is expected of them as part of managing MSIs and find out how much time they are spending doing so. You may not be able to change that, but some insight into costs of managing sustainability will help you to communicate relative ROI.

Regular engagement with stakeholders

Finding ways to regularly engage with stakeholders identified is vital. A full stakeholder engagement process is well beyond this guide, but many good ones are available, including the following:

- Doughty Centre's *Stakeholder Engagement: A Road Map to Meaningful Engagement*: http://www.som.cranfield.ac.uk/som/dinamic-content/media/CR%20Stakeholder.pdf

- BSR's *Back to Basics: How to Make Stakeholder Engagement Meaningful for Your Company*: http://www.bsr.org/reports/BSR_Five-Step_Guide_to_Stakeholder_Engagement.pdf

- *Critical Friends: The Emerging Role of Stakeholder Panels in Corporate Governance, Reporting and Assurance*: http://www.accountability.org/images/content/3/1/318/Critical%20Friends_StakeholderPanels_report.pdf

- Accountability's *AA1000SES Stakeholder Engagement Standard (2011)*: http://www.accountability.org/standards/aa1000ses/index.html

Audit

Different aspects of sustainability require various levels of trust. Increased levels of trust require increased transparency and increased reliability of data accuracy. In addition, data auditing can be used to clean up data for management purposes.

Marks & Spencer match their auditing of sustainability to their most material issues. Perhaps unusually, they give some priority to independent assurance based on importance to stakeholders, as shown in Figure 15.

FIGURE 15. Marks & Spencer's audit approach

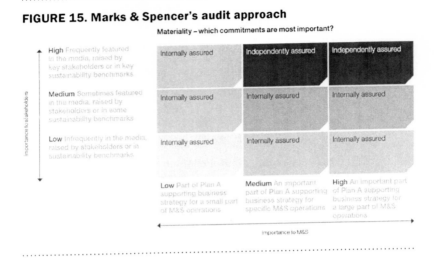

Materiality – which commitments are most important?

Supply chain

Guidance on supply chain issues and management, itself a very complex topic, is well beyond the scope of this book. For more guidance on managing your supply chain, see the following book in this series:

- *Building a Sustainable Supply Chain*

TELL

Before continuing, take a moment to find and read a really good sustainability report. Take a look at what someone else is doing and get inspired.

Take notes about what you like and don't like. Focus especially on what is believable and interesting (and what isn't).

If you don't know of a good report, then do a search on the web for 'sustainability report award' and read one or two that come up. Alternatively, download Marks & Spencer's latest 'How we do business' report (**http:// corporate.marksandspencer.com/howwedobusiness**), along with their 'Key lessons from Plan A business case' report. (**http://corporate.marksand spencer.com/documents/publications/2012/plan_a_report_2012.pdf**).

Of course, M&S's reports don't represent perfect sustainability reporting, but together they should give you some ideas about how to write an engaging sustainability report and some tips about how to make things happen behind the scenes to give the report and sustainability a good degree of credibility. In particular, you should be able to see how materiality of issues and commitment to understanding the costs and benefits have helped the organisation decide how to allocate resources in each area of sustainability.

Once again, a comprehensive review of how to use communications to embed and successfully integrate sustainability is beyond the scope of this guide. For other guidance, see the following books in this series:

- *Green Jujitsu*
- *Sustainability Reporting for SMEs*
- *Strategic Sustainability*

How to communicate and with whom

Having a sustainability report (including an integrated report) is not all that is required to communicate sustainability. An effective communications plan includes multiple channels and methods targeting appropriately segmented audiences.

If an issue owner of an MSI is doing good things, then brag about it internally.

In relation to external stakeholders, put yourself in their shoes and ask how you would like to hear back from your organisation.

All aspects of sustainability that are MSIs need at least an organisational comment or response. Perhaps the obvious spot for first communications is the website, which can easily be changed as and when things change. If you have identified other issues that will not be the subject of communications, then consider saying that. Something like, 'We are progressively targeting our most important sustainability issues and look forward to telling you more about our future plans.' If issues are currently not being managed then an identification of why that issue is important to the organisation's success will suffice.

Stakeholders engaged in the process will usually appreciate being told of their effect on the organisational approach and particularly how it has changed as a result of the engagement. But the opportunity to leverage communications on MSI goes well beyond specifically identified stakeholders.

Remember also that publication of sustainability communications is the beginning of conversations with stakeholders. Plan to re-engage with them off the back of publication of any sustainability reports or communiqués.

Connecting communications to materiality

Good sustainability reports will clearly set out the most relevant sustainability issues. Stakeholders who are interested in a particular issue should be able to quickly and easily find that issue. Matching reporting with stakeholder expectations is one of the advantages of a good materiality process after all! Responses to stakeholder concerns help to create trust, especially if there are multiple communication channels and types of communications. For the most important issues (MSIs), consider issuing self-contained communications which only deal with one issue.

Consider using your MSIs as headings for your report. It may be useful to use the sustainability framework chosen above as major headings and MSIs as sub-headings. The amount of space allocated to each issue should broadly reflect the relative importance of each MSI.

If possible, communicate why targeting each MSI creates value for the organisation, or why it might create value.

Credible communications

Aside from engaging on the most material sustainability issues, reports also need to have credibility. After all, the purpose of any reporting is to create trust; to help organisations to be as trusted as they want and/or need to be.

Your communications should actively highlight adherence to relevant standards where possible, and do so in a way that is clear and interesting.

If your organisation wants to be known as a sustainability leader then communications will also need to show how it is leading collaboration on the issue and teaching others about what it has learned.

Head versus heart

Some readers of your sustainability reports (not many I venture to suggest) look for a picture of children playing around a well/hydrant/football pitch/tablet and are happy that something good is being done. They love the tug at the heart of the story of one child's life which was changed by something good the organisation did.

Other readers look for numbers, audit trails and descriptions of where things didn't go to plan – a sure sign that the organisation is committed to learning from its mistakes.

You ultimately need to win both kinds of readers with your communications. Ideally that involves a good heart-tugging story along with numbers of how many people have benefitted or how much additional value has been created.

An overly simple communications framework

If your organisation is going to say that it is sustainable, then it needs to be able to show how it is being so. In a social media world, not many people believe things that organisations say, unless they have first generated trust (or at least not given reasons to bring trust into question).

FIGURE 16. Simple sustainability communications analyser.

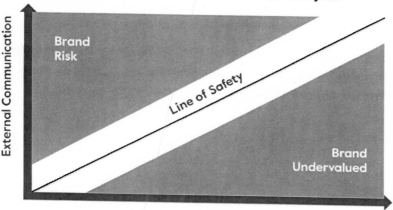

Figure 16 is a simple diagram that conveys how effective communications on sustainability issues will be in relation to brand value. Organisations that brag too much about their sustainability and don't perform in a way that meets the expectations of trust are very likely to be in the 'brand risk' area of the graph. Organisations that do well on sustainability but don't talk about it are missing out on trust and are very likely to be in the 'brand undervalued' area.

Your goal should be to ensure that your sustainability communications stay close to the (somewhat mythical) 'line of safety'. It is also important to understand that the baseline of expected sustainability performance is continuing to rise.

Benchmarking

If your organisation is reporting its MSIs, then at some point it needs to understand how others are performing on the same issues. The cursory scan of issues mentioned in the Scan stage isn't really enough to do a comparative analysis of the *quality* of reporting on your MSIs.

In order for your communications to be credible, a more thorough analysis needs to be undertaken so that your organisation appreciates where the minimum expectations are in terms of sustainability reporting.

CHECKLIST: PART 2 – HOW

SCAN

- [ ] Pick a framework suitable for your organisation to use
- [ ] Gather relevant Organisational tools and frameworks
- [ ] Prepare a Sustainable Issues Record (long list) using:
  - Current Business Tools
  - Internal views on Sustainability
  - Views of External Stakeholders
  - External standards and comparators

PRIORITISE

- [ ] Consolidate and clarify
- [ ] Identify Importance to Stakeholders
- [ ] Identify Importance to Organisation
  - ADD other factors (if desired)
- [ ] Finalise Materiality scores
- [ ] Create a Materiality Matrix (and make it visually appealing)
- [ ] Sense Check Conclusions

EMBED

- [ ] Do a Gap Analysis of the SIR
- [ ] Find owners and fill gaps
- [ ] Integrate MSIs into the Risk Register

- [ ] Measure legacy costs and plan to measure new metrics
- [ ] Identify targets and metrics for MSIs
- [ ] Schedule next year's sustainability summit

MANAGE

- [ ] Match internal sustainability processes with regular organisational processes
- [ ] Identify 'Quick Wins'
- [ ] Support the owners of MSIs
- [ ] Engage with Stakeholders Regularly
  - Encourage relationship owners to do the engaging
- [ ] Consider auditing the most important MSIs
- [ ] Construct an appropriate supply chain process
- [ ] Start building the Business Case for Sustainability

TELL

- [ ] Make it interesting
- [ ] Communicate Performance and Tell a good story
- [ ] Get stakeholder feedback (internal and external)
- [ ] Keep it on the Line of Safety

REPEAT

Conclusion

THE MODEL OF MATERIALITY PROCESS put forward in this book is something of a compromise. Strictly speaking it needs some adaptation (although fairly minimal) to be compliant with the reporting obligations related to IIRC and GRI's G4.

It is also well beyond what would be required by SASB. But it isn't beyond the expectations of many stakeholders, and can help organisations to create more value for shareholders and stakeholders alike.

Of course, the demands of each of those audiences aren't the same, but that's not really the point. The point is to understand organisations in the broader context of civil society and the relationships that they have with a wide variety of actors. The model firmly preserves that concept while blending it with the interests of the organisation performing the analysis.

We're all better off when companies create approaches that work in the real world.[9]

Pragmatism has won a lot of victories in the quest for increased CSR/ sustainability/responsible business and it is the goal of the author for the approach detailed to be pragmatic, if not perfect.

More (or less) informed readers might criticise this book because it doesn't agree at all points with their preferred method of identifying material issues. But the model is flexible enough to accommodate various frameworks and situations, and will help companies meet

CONCLUSION

the expectations of investors, providers of other financial capital and stakeholders.

A final reminder: the key goal of any of these types of processes is to build credibility and trust for the organisation.

....

APPENDIX A

Sustainability Team Questions

10 QUESTIONS TO ASK SUSTAINABILITY TEAM MEMBERS

1. What do you understand by the term 'sustainability'?

2. How is sustainability connected to your role?

3. What are your teams' KPIs?

4. What metrics do you have already that could be used to measure sustainability?

5. What metrics could you put in place to measure sustainability?

6. Who are your most important stakeholders?

7. Where can our organisation have its best sustainability impacts?

8. Where does our organisation have its worst sustainability impacts?

9. What should we be famous for in sustainability?

10. Who should be involved in our sustainability programme?

APPENDIX B

Sustainability Issues Record

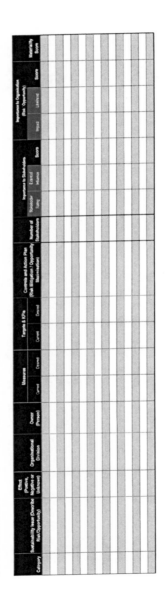

Common Material Sustainability Issues

ALL SUSTAINABILITY ISSUES scoring an average rating by stakeholders and organisations of greater than 5 out of 10 from research conducted by Fronesys in 2011. More details are available in the research report's publicly available executive summary: **http://www.fronesys.com/Reports/ Determining-Materiality-white-paper-from-Fronesys.pdf**

Issues are listed in alphabetical order.

bold   Top ten issues

*   Items added by the author

- access to goods and services*
- biodiversity
- bribery and corruption
- **climate change effects**
- carbon emissions/footprint
- community engagement/investment
- compensation
- corporate governance
- customer inclusion

- **customer relationships/satisfaction**
- dangerous chemical use
- demographic change
- diversity
- economic contribution
- **economic development**
- **economic stability**
- education and skills
- employee development
- **employee retention and attraction**
- employee satisfaction
- employee volunteering
- embedded carbon*
- **energy use**
- environmental protection
- ethics/integrity
- executive pay
- fair trade*
- freedom of association
- **greenhouse gas emissions**
- governance and ethics*
- hazardous chemicals
- health and safety
- human rights

- indigenous rights*
- innovation
- land use
- **legal compliance**
- life cycle analysis
- low carbon alternatives*
- local community stability*
- local economic development
- packaging
- pollutants
- price fairness*
- privacy
- product durability*
- product recyclability*
- product use/educating consumers*
- **product safety**
- product transparency*
- productivity*
- public policy positions
- recycling
- renewable energy
- resource use/efficiency
- responsible procurement
- responsible selling and marketing

- resources recycled*
- resources used*
- restructuring/downsizing
- social impact*
- social return on investment*
- stakeholder engagement
- supplier performance
- **sustainable products**
- sustainable sourcing*
- talent attraction*
- transport/fleet emissions
- waste
- water consumption
- work–life balance and wellness

As discussed above, this list should be used to identify categories of more specific issues for use in your materiality process.

APPENDIX D

Further Resources

Primary resources

Dō Sustainability

Understanding G4 (Elaine Cohen)

Dō Sustainability's *Understanding G4* also briefly deals with materiality, although not in any significant detail. For many professionals, this book will be a companion volume to the G4 guide.

The author

Article with tips on making materiality work in your organisation: http://www.dwaynebaraka.com/blog/2013/05/07/top-tip-master-materiality-making-csr-look-easy/

Article on materiality, transparency and comparability and how they aren't the same thing: http://www.dwaynebaraka.com/blog/2013/06/17/gris-g4-materiality-transparency-comparability-fight/

Free resources (including on materiality) from valuecsr: http://www.valuecsr.com/free-resources/#

Mastering the materiality matrix: http://valuecsr.com/wp-content/uploads/2013/05/Materiality-Matrix-Top-Tips-Final.pdf

Defining materiality: http://www.dwaynebaraka.com/blog/2014/01/27/defining-materiality/

APPENDIX D:
FURTHER RESOURCES

Materiality matrix: examples from Ford, Intel and Electrolux: http://www.dwaynebaraka.com/blog/2014/01/11/materiality-matrix-more-examples/

GRI's materials relating to G3 and G4:

G3 reporting guidelines: https://www.globalreporting.org/reporting/G3andg3-1/guidelines-online/TechnicalProtocol/Pages/MaterialityInTheContextOfTheGRIReportingFramework.aspx

G3 guide to materiality: https://www.globalreporting.org/resourcelibrary/Materiality.pdf

G4 introduction: https://www.globalreporting.org/reporting/g4/Pages/default.aspx

G4 Part 1 – reporting principles and standard disclosures: https://www.globalreporting.org/resourcelibrary/GRIG4-Part1-Reporting-Principles-and-Standard-Disclosures.pdf

G4 Part 2 – implementation manual: https://www.globalreporting.org/resourcelibrary/GRIG4-Part2-Implementation-Manual.pdf

International Integrated Reporting Council

The International <IR> Framework (2013): http://www.theiirc.org/international-ir-framework/

Materiality Background Paper for <IR> (2013): http://www.theiirc.org/wp-content/uploads/2013/03/IR-Background-Paper-Materiality.pdf

Sustainability Accounting Standards Board

Materiality principles: http://www.sasb.org/approach/principles/

Definition and importance: http://www.sasb.org/materiality/important/

Other resources

AccountAbility

The Materiality Report: Aligning Strategy, Performance and Reporting: A Briefing (2003): http://www.accountability.org/images/content/2/0/202.pdf

The Materiality Report: Aligning Strategy, Performance and Reporting (2006): http://www.accountability.org/about-us/publications/materiality.html

Redefining Materiality II: Why it Matters, Who's Involved, and What It Means for Corporate Leaders and Boards (2013): http://www.accountability.org/images/content/6/8/686/AA_Materiality_Report_Aug2013 FINAL.pdf

Critical Friends: The Emerging Role of Stakeholder Panels in Corporate Governance, Reporting and Assurance (2007) (co-authored with entopies): http://www.accountability.org/images/content/3/1/318/Critical%20Friends_StakeholderPanels_report.pdf

Banarra Consulting

Materiality – Unlocking Its Potential for Reporting and Business Improvement (2013): http://paul-banarra.tumblr.com/post/66334169264 (accessed 11 November 2013)

BSR

Navigating the Materiality Muddle (2013): http://www.bsr.org/en/our-insights/bsr-insight-article/navigating-the-materiality-muddle

APPENDIX D:
FURTHER RESOURCES

Brown Flynn

Getting Materiality Right: A Whitepaper (2013): http://www.brownflynn.com/gettingmaterialityright.asp

Corporate Citizenship

Materiality (2013): http://www.corporate-citizenship.com/wp-content/uploads/Corporate-Citizenship-Materiality.pdfa

Elaine Cohen

Blog post looking a many varieties of materiality with a focus on matrices (2011) – remarkably relevant today: http://csr-reporting.blogspot.co.uk/2011/10/31-ways-of-looking-at-materiality.html

Blog looking at the consequences of materiality for organisations: http://csr-reporting.blogspot.co.uk/2013/07/g4-that-materiality-thing-again.html

Cranfield University's Doughty Centre for Corporate Responsibility

How to Identify Impacts (2013): http://www.som.cranfield.ac.uk/som/p17711/Knowledge-Interchange/Management-Themes/Corporate-Responsibility-and-Sustainability/Corporate-Responsibility-and-Sustainability-News/How-to-identify-impacts

Fronesys

Materiality Futures: http://www.fronesys.com/blog/materiality-futures-fronesys-report.html

Framework

The Materiality Bridge – A Study of Correlation of Materiality Matrices with GRI G3 Reporting: http://framework-llc.com/the-materiality-bridge-2/

Academic articles

Eccles, R.G., Krzus, M.P., Rogers, J. and Serafeim, G. 2012. The need for sector-specific materiality and sustainability reporting standards. *Journal of Applied Corporate Finance* (Volume 24): 65–71. doi: 10.1111/j.1745-6622.2012.00380.x http://www.sasb.org/wp-content/uploads/2012/06/JACF-Sector-Materiality.pdf

Ioannou, I. and Serafeim, G. 2012. The consequences of mandatory corporate sustainability reporting. Harvard Business School Working Paper, No. 11-100. http://www.hbs.edu/faculty/Publication%20Files/11-100_35684ae7-fcdc-4aae-9626-de4b2acb1748.pdf

Lyndberg, S., Rogers, J. and Wood, D. 2010. From transparency to performance: industry-based sustainability reporting on key issues. The Hauser Centre for Non-Profit Organisations. http://www.sasb.org/wp-content/uploads/2012/03/IRI_Transparency-to-Performance.pdf

Notes

1. Brown Flynn (2013). See Appendix D.

2. Probably first used in Jonathon Porritt's 2007 book *Capitalism as if the World Matters*. London and New York: Routledge.

3. During a TED Talk: **http://www.ted.com/talks/elon_musk_the_mind_behind_tesla_spacex_solarcity.html** (accessed 1 November 2013).

4. Accountability 2013. See Appendix D.

5. Paul Davies, Banarra Consulting (2013). See Appendix D.

6. Almost anyone who has ever completed an MBA knows this management-ism.

7. This diagram is based on a materiality process diagram by Banarra Consulting (2013). See Appendix D.

8. Cranfield University (2013), p. 31. See Appendix D.

9. BSR (2013). See Appendix D.

Lightning Source UK Ltd.
Milton Keynes UK
UKOW04f2055200214

226858UK00001B/1/P